GARDEN OF MIRACLES

"Thy Word have I hid in mine heart

BIBLE MEMORY ASSOCIATION

Presented by the

Bible Memory Association Int.

ST LOUIS, MISSOURI

To

BECKY
CRAGOE

AS A REWARD
for memorizing Scripture
in the annual Contest

that I might not sin against Thee."

GARDEN
OF
MIRACLES

*A history of the
African Inland Mission*

by
KENNETH RICHARDSON

Published in association with the
AFRICA INLAND MISSION by

VICTORY PRESS
LONDON AND EASTBOURNE

SBN 85476 007 5

Printed in Great Britain for
VICTORY PRESS (Evangelical Publishers Ltd.)
Lottbridge Drove, Eastbourne, Sussex
by Richard Clay (The Chaucer Press) Ltd.
Bungay, Suffolk

Foreword

A GARDEN is a miracle. Indeed, it is a whole mass of miracles. It is part of an infinite series of miracles.

To begin with, think of the soil. If seed of even the highest quality were planted in the dust of the desert, it would show no more signs of life than the grains of sand around it. Good soil is only produced by miracles. Many natural agencies work together to bring about the chemical changes necessary to cause the seed to germinate and the tender plant to grow.

Then again, consider the seed. Apparently dead, it explodes into life when planted under the right conditions. Out of that dry 'bare grain' spring flowers, trees, vegetables 'as it hath pleased Him', in infinite variety of colour, shape, scent, size and use. Miracle indeed!

Contemplate all the forces of climate and disease ranged against the life of seed and plant. And, in addition, there is insatiable hunger of the wilderness to regain that which has been wrenched from its grasp. The fact that any seed endures is a miracle.

Man must do his work, reclaiming and preparing the ground. The gardener must sow the seed, tend and water it. But all the efforts of man will come to nought unless God works in miracle, preparing the soil, governing the elements, controlling the adversaries and quickening the seed.

When man, who is himself such a bundle of miracles, plants a garden, with all its miracle, he is touching eternity. He is doing his necessary, but minor, part in producing myriads of unborn harvests stretching on into endless reaches of the future.

But a garden is a parable of still greater miracles. The Lord's gardeners go forth, break the ground, scatter the precious seed of the Word of God, water and tend it; and see it spring up, blossom and bear fruit. But it is God who performs the miracle. Spiritual truths are spiritually discerned, and only the Spirit of God can bring it about. All the art and technique of the preacher can never produce it. His pressure and persuasiveness may do more harm than good. But when God sets to work, life and fruit appear.

The following pages tell of miracles which have been seen and are still taking place in Africa. The fewness of the labourers, the difficulties which have been encountered and the opposition of an implacable foe have but thrown into greater relief the immensity of the miracles which have been wrought by the Lord of the Harvest.

As in the earthly counterpart, the results produced are part of an eternal process, for the fruit produced in the spiritual garden has in it the means of self-propagation, the seed of countless harvests stretching on into eternity.

It has been possible to mention only a few of the most prominent of those who have toiled in this garden. Much has had to be omitted. The full record is in Heaven, and many servants who have not been given a place in this record will be remembered in that Day. Many have made their contribution from afar. They have watered the seed with their prayers and have surrounded the tender plants with their fervent intercessions; they have given of their substance. Their part in the great harvest will be shown clearly 'when the mists have rolled away'.

Contents

Chronology

Kikuyu Conference, Kenya

1914 Githumu opened (Kenya)
      [4th August] First World War commenced
      Nandi work (Kenya) started at Chebusas

1915 Work opened at Bafuka (Napopo), Yakaluku, Ara, Adza
      (Congo)
      Mulango (Kenya) taken over from Leipsig Lutherian Mission

1917 Ter Akara (Congo) opened

1918 Work started in West Nile District, Uganda, at Arua
      Stations opened at Kisani, Kapsabet and Siyapei (Kenya)
      and at Aba, Rabu, Blukwa, Bogoro, Aru (Congo)

1919 Work commenced at Lumbwa (Kenya) and Moto (Congo)

1920 Stations opened at Linga, Rethy and Moldisa (Todro) in
      Congo

1922 Work commenced at Luhumbo (Tanzania)

1924 Stations opened at Adi (Congo) and Zemio (Central African
      Republic)

1925 Nandi work (Kenya) transferred to Kapsabet from Chebesas
      Stations opened at Rafai and Djema (Central African
      Republic)
      C. E. Hurlburt resigned

1926 Work opened at Kabartonjo (Kenya) and Buduhe (Tan-
      zania)

1929 Goli station (Uganda) opened

1930 Work commenced at Eldoret (Kenya)

1931 Stations opened at Banda (Congo), Mwanza (Tanzania) and
      Kericho (Kenya)

1932 Maitulu, Asa, Ruwenzori (Mwenda) and Oicha opened in
      Congo

1933 Work commenced at Aungba (Congo), Lasit (Loitokitok)
      and Kapsowar (Kenya)

1934 Ogada (Kenya) taken over by A.I.M.
      Uzinza and Katungulu opened in Tanzania.

1935 Work opened at Kingyang (Kenya)

1937 Work commenced on Ukerewe Island (Tanzania) and Tambach (Kessup, Kenya)

1938 Ntuzu station opened (Tanzania)

1939 Second World War commenced

1940 Work commenced at Moyo (Uganda)

1942 Butundwe (Tanzania) opened

1948 Work commenced at Ukara Island (Tanzania)

1949 Entrance to Southern Sudan. Opari opened

1950 Work started at Kuluva (Uganda)

1955 Jubilee Year of Mission. New Constitution adopted. R. T. Davis appointed first International Secretary (later called General Director)

K. L. Downing appointed first General Field Secretary

1959 Station opened at Lokori (Kenya)

1962 Resignation of R. T. Davis as General Director

1963 [19th August] Homecall of R. T. Davis
All missionaries expelled from Southern Sudan

1964 All missionaries evacuated from N.E. Congo
Work commenced at Nyabirongo (Uganda)

1965 Kaptagat (Kenya) opened as Conference Centre

1966 Missionaries return to Congo
Nyachogochogo (Kenya) opened

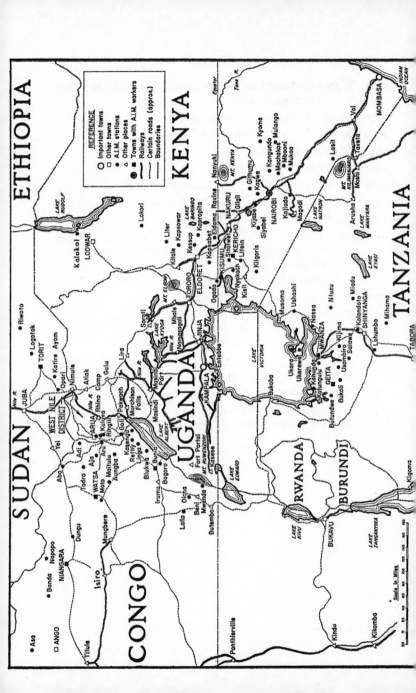

This map shows most of the main stations of the A.I.M. with the exception of those in the CENTRAL AFRICAN REPUBLIC—north of Congo and west of Sudan—OBO, ZEMIO, RAFAI and DJEMA.

Since the map was prepared two stations—GATAB and LOGLOGO have been opened in the Northern Frontier District of Kenya, and NYACHOGOCHOGO in the south, near Kisii and the border with Tanzania.

KAGANDO (formerly Nyabirongo) is near Kasese in Western Uganda.

The Centre Médical Evangelique is at NYANKUNDE, south of Bunia in Congo.

PART ONE

PLOUGHING IN HOPE

I

The Unclaimed Wilderness

AFRICA was already hitting the headlines of the newspapers in the leisurely 1890s. The ordinary reader turned to his atlas to find out where the strange places could be found. He had to run his eyes halfway down the east coast of Africa before he could find Mombasa, with its huge natural harbour. So the unknown continent began to take definite shape in his mind.

The Governments knew where these places were, however, for they had their eye on them. Portugal had long had her colonies; Belgium had Congo; and Germany, France and Great Britain were grasping for other parts.

But the people mainly concerned, the 230 millions of inhabitants of that vast continent, were quite unconscious of the worldwide interest which was centred on them. The giant was still asleep.

Some of them had caught a glimpse of white faces. A few explorers had made their hazardous way into the centre; Livingstone had made his famous safaris; Stanley had made history by his travels; forts manned by Europeans had been established here and there; a few widely separated mission stations had been opened. But in the main 'darkness, gross darkness' covered the land.

Although the inhabitants were completely ignorant of the great outside world, they were far from backward along their own lines. They had expert knowledge of the trees and plants which surrounded them, and of the habits of the wild animals which shared the countryside with them. The newcomers followed with amazement as these Africans tracked the game through the jungle. Their sense of direction was uncanny, and their powers of observation astounding. Their memories, unencumbered by book learning, were prodigious. They possessed natural wisdom in judgment. Cheerfulness and humour were characteristics and they were born mimics.

True, the explanations of the various phases of nature and natural phenomena were associated with magic, or spirits, or other forms of animism; but this satisfied them. It had to, for they knew nothing of the findings of science. No illness was attributed to natural causes. It was caused by poison, or a curse, or the evil eye or offended spirits.

There was practically nothing by way of invention. It never entered the heads of even the most advanced to write. Their clothing was primeval. Many tribes wore none; others dressed themselves in bark-cloth or animal skins.

As for religion, they were animists. Mohammedanism had spread along the coasts, but inland the tribes were still pagan. They had vague ideas of a Supreme Being but He was far off and they knew little about Him. They believed in a life after death and another world; but it was all dim, shadowy and undefined. It was peopled by spirits. Some were the spirits of their ancestors, still haunting the old places they had inhabited. Others were good or bad spirits. All these must be placated by offerings or sacrifices, for they were very easily offended and if neglected could cause calamity or death.

Hence the most important man was the witch-doctor. He, or she—for some were women—could make contact with the spirits. In fact, he was a spirit medium. He had a familiar spirit. The Old Testament phrase 'wizards that peep and mutter' is an exact description. He could divine. He was consulted in all cases of disease or calamity, and when important decisions had to be made.

The witch-doctor often had a knowledge of herbal remedies which was useful. This knowledge was shared by the older women. It was sometimes put to more sinister use; for there were deadly poisons, and the heads of arrows were dipped into them to ensure the death of any who were wounded by them. They acted with great rapidity. The witch-doctors also sold charms and amulets. In consideration for large payment they would provide a talisman to tie on the wrist or hang round the neck to ward off attacks of the spirits and to safeguard health.

Next to the witch-doctor the rain-maker was perhaps the most important person. He was a kind of priest called upon in time of drought to propitiate the spirits responsible for making rain. Near the site of Adi station there was a rock which was said to be the abode of the rain-spirit. In time of severe drought a gathering would take place and the chief rain-makers would perform their sacrificial rites in the expectation that rain would be given.

The villages consisted of the houses of one family. They were mud huts, usually thatched and circular in shape. Near by was a kraal for cattle; or among certain tribes, the animals shared the hut with the family. Their cattle were their wealth. With them they paid the bride-price, met the demands of the witch-doctors or bargained for other commodities.

The territory which is now known as the Republic of Kenya was called British East Africa at the time when Peter Cameron Scott first landed there. It straddles the Equator and stretches from the Indian Ocean and the Somali Republic on the east to Lake Victoria and Uganda on the west, and the Sudan on the north-west. The Republic of Tanzania lies to the south.

The most fertile soil and the most temperate climate are found in the highlands. These are reached near Nairobi —about 300 miles inland. They are divided by the great Rift Valley which stretches across Kenya and can be traced throughout a large part of Africa. In the north of Kenya it is only a shallow depression and Lake Rudolf lies in it; but farther south the Rift is deeper and about 40 miles wide. Its sides are formidable escarpments.

Kenya's area is approximately 225,000 square miles— about as large as France. Its population today is a little under 9 million. The Africans belong to four main language groups: Bantu, Nilo-Hamitic, Nilotic and Hamitic. The Bantu form the largest group and it includes the Kikuyu, Kamba and a number of other tribes. The Nilo-Hamitic include Maasai, Nandi, Kipsigis, Turkana, Pokot and Samburu. The Luo tribe is Nilotic—the only one in Kenya, and is related to the Acholi and Alur tribes in Uganda. These people live around the Kavirondo Gulf of Lake Victoria. The only representatives of the Hamitic group are the Somalis who are found mainly in the north-eastern corner. They are nomads, their wealth consisting of camels and other livestock.

Such then are the country and peoples in which the Africa Inland Mission opened work in 1895.

2

A Corn of Wheat

PETER CAMERON SCOTT

THE founding of the Africa Inland Mission by Peter Cameron Scott in 1895 was the culmination of a series of experiences by which the Lord had been preparing him for his main task.

He was born in Glasgow on 7th March 1867 of godly parents. When some years later they decided to emigrate to America they left behind the grave of a beloved daughter. They settled in Philadelphia. Peter had a good voice and was fortunate to be able to have it trained under an Italian maestro. He was invited to sing professionally, but, to his great disappointment, his parents would not hear of it, sensing the dangers inherent in such a career.

He turned from the enchanting vision of fame to work in a printer's office. When he was twenty, a severe breakdown in health led the doctor to advise that he return to Scotland in the hope that he might benefit from the change of climate.

While there he visited the cemetery where his sister had been laid to rest. As he stood over the grave, he meditated on the possibility of his own death, and promised God that if his life were spared it should be lived 'henceforth ... unto Him'. God took him at his word. His health began to improve and by the following year he was able to return to America and resume the work he left. This was probably the first time Peter had really surrendered to the Lord. It was a peak experience.

But his resolution began to pale. He had come of age by this time and felt that he was free to control his own movements. He caught sight of an advertisement for chorus-singers in an opera and was immediately attracted to it. So he set out to offer his services.

For some time prior to this he had been haunted by a special text of Scripture:

'Ye are not your own, ye are bought with a price: therefore glorify God in your body and your spirit which are God's' (1 Cor. 6 : 19, 20).

This pricked his conscience, and tormented him to such an extent that on one occasion he tried to erase it from his Bible!

As he mounted the steps of the Opera House to respond to the advertisement, the Holy Spirit again reminded him of the text.

'Are you going to glorify God by going in there?' the 'still, small voice' asked.

But he was determined, and pressed on up the steps. Suddenly, however, a wave of conviction swept over him. He turned abruptly and walked away. As he did so, peace flooded his soul.

'Lord,' said he, 'I will never go into such a place again.' And he never did.

It was a moment of surrender. From that time forward, God was the absolute Master of Peter Cameron Scott.

The crisis through which he had passed led him to trust the Lord, not only for spiritual health but for physical restoration as well. His condition improved remarkably.

This, however, was secondary. His gaze was fixed upon

the Lord, and he was more taken up with the spiritual enrichment which had come to him than with the physical healing. The love of the world was displaced by an intense desire to tell others of the love of the Saviour.

It was at this time that the Holy Spirit directed his thoughts to Africa, where millions were without the knowledge of Christ. Yet at first he rejected the thought of working there. The climate was deadly and he would have to face the difficulties of language.

Wherever it might be, however, he determined to take up training which would fit him for whole-time service for his Master. He entered the New York Missionary Training College. In order to support himself during the period of training, he worked from three to seven hours daily at his former business. What spare time he could find he spent in the slums pointing desperate characters to Christ, trusting God for their conversion.

Increasingly the burden of Africa weighed upon his heart. He gave three weeks to earnest prayer that he might know the Lord's will. At the end of that time, guidance having become clearer, he wrote to his parents telling them how he was being led, and seeking their approval for the step he proposed to take. A loving reply from his mother by return post said:

'The day you left home to go to the College, going to my room, on my knees I gave you up more than ever to the Lord to go wherever He might call you.'

Before their birth, this devoted mother had dedicated each of her children to the Lord.

This word confirmed the leading. He was accepted by the International Missionary Alliance for service on the

West Coast of Africa, and sailed in November 1890.

The intervening months were filled with diligent efforts to win the lost. He was used to the conversion of the delinquent son of a Presbyterian elder who had strayed so far that he felt he was beyond the reach of God's mercy. Peter had a strange hold over men, and was given respectful attention, even by drunkards.

Scott was slight of frame, of medium height and weight. He was impressive in appearance, having regular features, high forehead surmounted by heavy dark hair. His manner was gentlemanly, his demeanour mild. At the same time, under that kid-glove exterior, there was a firmness which could hit out hard for the right.

At an impressive service conducted by Rev. A. B. Simpson in New York, Scott was ordained the day before he sailed. His mother accompanied him as far as London.

On the morning of 31st January 1891 the ship anchored off the port of Banana at the mouth of the Congo River. Peter landed and went inland to the field of the Missionary Alliance.

His brother John joined him a few months later and they looked forward to united service for the Lord. But God had other plans and, after a short time on the field, John passed away. With his own hands Peter made the coffin, dug the grave and laid to rest the one he described as 'a gentle, loving and self-sacrificing brother'. Here he reached another crisis. Alone at his brother's grave, he dedicated himself afresh to the work of preaching the Gospel in Africa.

But Peter Scott himself was not given many months in which to work there. Repeated attacks of fever sapped his strength until he had to leave the country.

He travelled home by way of England and stayed for a

while with his friends Mr. and Mrs. Brodie in London. They always remembered his arrival at their house. It was a foggy November evening. They were entertaining a few outgoing missionaries. Full of enthusiasm, the young people were singing hymns. In the midst of it a cab drew up and a pathetic figure was helped out. Supported by a strong arm he entered the room and sat down among the outgoing recruits. His appearance showed the scars of his experiences, but it was obvious that he had come into a deeper knowledge of God. Looking round at the new missionaries he said:

'Well, friends, you are going forth—I have come back. It is no child's play; it is a battle!'

While in London Peter had time to commune with God and he gained fresh spiritual strength. He was greatly helped by attending a prayer meeting of the China Inland Mission.

He found it hard to be idle, and the urgent needs of Africa pressed heavily upon him. He would pace the floor saying, 'I must go! I must go! They are perishing!' Both in America and England he worked continuously, stressing the need for more missionaries to preach the Gospel to the millions of souls in darkness.

East and Central Africa was a strategic area. If only the Gospel could be preached there, it might prove a barrier to Mohammedanism and bring light to millions of Africans tormented by fear, lost in sin. Here was a piece of wilderness which should be reclaimed and made a garden of the Lord.

His health, not yet fully restored, suffered a serious setback, and there were doubts whether he would recover. He was painfully aware of the enormous need, yet he could do nothing. It brought him to an end of himself.

But that is just where God meets a man. His friends

Mr. and Mrs. Brodie nursed him back to health in their home and gave him every care.

One day, during his convalescence, Mrs. Brodie took him to Westminster Abbey. They came to the tomb of 'David Livingstone: Missionary, Philanthropist, Explorer'. Reverently he knelt.

The sight of a young man kneeling there may have called forth passing comment by the sightseers who wandered through the historic building; but it was soon forgotten. Yet to Peter, as he knelt there and read the words: 'Other sheep I have which are not of this fold; them also I must bring' (John 10 : 16), there came a definite sense of call and commission. He gave himself afresh to the Lord and heard the divine call to continue where Livingstone had laid down his task. Those few moments crystallized the thoughts which had been coursing through his mind during recent weeks—a line of mission stations, some 2,000 miles in length, across Africa from the East to Lake Chad in the centre. The seed of the Africa Inland Mission had been planted.

Mrs. Brodie touched his shoulder and recalled him to his surroundings. And the unsuspecting sightseers went on their way. It was the final crisis in his preparation.

Thus we see and marvel at God's dealings as He moulded this life for His service and took the first outward steps towards the planting of a fruitful garden in East Africa.

Peter returned to America, eager to pass the burden on to others. Many were stirred by his ministry.

He met Dr. A. T. Pierson and told him of the vision which had been given to him of a line of mission stations through East and Central Africa. Dr. Pierson gave him much encouragement and a committee was formed. The Rev. C. E. Hurlburt, who was to play such an important part later, was a member of it.

It seemed an inopportune time for the launching of a

new missionary society. Many organizations already existing were in debt and unable to expand. Yet Peter
Cameron Scott was convinced that, if this was of God,
He would supply their needs. The whole project was committed to God in prayer. Resting on the promises of God,
they looked to Him alone. No appeals for money were
made, nor any debt incurred. The decision to adopt this
principle was made after much thought and prayer. It has
been a governing principle of the Mission ever since. There
have been times of shortage, but there has never been a
time when God has failed to fulfil His promise.

In answer to prayer, one and another offered for the
Lord's service in Africa. Among them was Peter's sister,
Margaret. A farewell service for the first party of eight
was held in August 1895 at the Pennsylvania Bible Institute in Philadelphia which, at the same time, was dedicated
to the Lord as the headquarters of the Mission. In many
wonderful ways money was provided for passages and
outfits, and a surplus for other needs which might arise.

Further interest in the new Mission was aroused as the
workers gave their testimonies when they travelled by way
of Scotland.

Once again Peter's mother accompanied her two
children part of the way. She left them in Paris. Here, on
the very day of their departure, the sad news was received
of the homecall of another brother, George. Through this
event God spoke to Mrs. Scott, convincing her that He
wanted her, as well as the remaining members of the
family, to leave all and serve Him in Africa. This they did
later.

The party reached the island of Zanzibar in October, at
the end of a voyage in which there had been many evi-
dences of God's care. It was a thrilling experience to steam
into the ancient harbour.

From the sea, Zanzibar presented much the same appearance as it does today. The deep blue sea splashes lazily on white coral beaches and the air is heavy with the scent of cloves. How interesting they would have found the Arab dhows loading or unloading at the quays. These craft are still built locally. Each has one tall mast with a huge triangular sail and a very long bowsprit.

Looking towards the town, the Sultan's Palace and other important buildings can be seen, all foursquare and built of grey coral. The minarets of the mosques stand out, and from them the call to prayer is sounded.

Once on shore, the place is crammed full of interest. The crooked, narrow streets are trodden by an endless stream of Arabs, Negroes and people from many other eastern countries. Cattle and donkeys thread their way through the jostling crowds. Behind the brass-studded doors which bar access to the solidly built houses, live wealthy Arabs with their huge harems, and, even in those late days, they still had their retinues of slaves. True, the old slave market had been closed over twenty years before and an Anglican cathedral erected in its place; but much traffic in slaves was carried on surreptitiously.

Merchandise from all over the East can still be bought in the bazaars, pervaded with the scent of spices of all kinds. Beyond the town are the clove plantations for which the island is famous, and from which the whole world is supplied.

There the party disembarked. A few days later, Peter Scott and Mr. Kreiger, one of the other men in the party, crossed over to Mombasa to make arrangements for the journey inland.

The territory near the coast had already been occupied by other missions (the Church Missionary Society, the German Lutheran Mission and the Methodist Mission), and Peter Scott's vision had been 'to preach the Gospel not where Christ was named, lest I should build upon another man's foundation' (Rom. 15 : 20). His desire was to go to the unreached tribes of the interior. Not for nought had the Mission been called 'The Africa *Inland* Mission'.

The Lord prospered their way, and suitable agents to forward supplies were found. The Church Missionary Society graciously provided a house wherein the ladies of the party could live until the way should open for them to go inland. Porters were recruited for the long journey the men were to make. So the whole party came over to Mombasa.

On 15th November four of the men, reassured by tokens of the Lord's smile on their project, set out to find a base for their work. The other man of the party remained at Mombasa to take care of the ladies.

Some years later Mr. Hurlburt wrote the following description of the country through which these pioneers had to pass:

'The coast region of East Africa is watered by mists driven in from the sea, and is very fertile, producing coconuts, bananas, mangoes, pineapples and vegetables. But one hundred miles inland this fruitfulness is lost in the Taru Desert, about sixty miles wide, where frequently no rain falls for several years at a time. Passing this desert, the country rises rapidly to the hill region, ranging from three to eight or nine thousand feet high, finding its northern climax in Mt. Kenia, just at the equator, 18,600 feet above the sea level; and its southern climax in Kilima Njaro, which raises its lofty head on the dividing line between the British and German Protectorates over 19,000 feet high. Both these mountains are perpetually snow-crowned and hence exert a marked influence upon the otherwise torrid climate of eastern equatorial Africa.'

Their force when they set forth numbered about three hundred men and they had with them forty-two camels. An Arab chief, Mbaruk, had rebelled and was causing trouble, and a military escort under a European officer was necessary to see them safely through the area of danger.

Safari in those days was a precarious undertaking. The first part of the journey was through low-lying and very humid country. Wearing the huge helmets and heavy spine pads which were then deemed necessary for protection from the tropical sun, the four men tramped on.

A hard dry scrub stretched away in the distance, and the huts looked very unromantic—flat-roofed mud-and-wattle boxes. Here and there on the plain, groups of huge baobab trees still attract attention.

On the second day of their journey they passed through the territory of the rebellious chief and they were grateful for the protection afforded by their military escort. During the night they were awakened by shots fired into the camp by some of the rebels, but no harm was done.

As they resumed their safari they were faced with a long waterless stretch and they decided to journey by night. Within a day or two, however, they were heartened by rain. They hurried on to Mazima Matatu (Three Wells), but they found no water there. They therefore pressed on to Maungu Dogo, a hill about 3,000 feet high, where they encamped, having found a supply of water.

Scott and one of the others shot antelope so that they did not lack for meat.

As the rains set in, they were faced with swollen rivers and swamps. His servant offered to carry Peter across one of these, but he plunged into a hole and they were both soaked. This brought on a heavy chill which laid Scott low.

There were other hazards too. Insect pests multiplied, and they were annoyed by mosquitoes. As a result of this

they suffered from malaria. Several times they encountered lions, and once or twice rhinoceroses attacked
the party.

By 12th December they had reached more promising
country near Mount Nzawi, 6,000 feet high, where there
were fertile valleys and cultivated patches. The villages,
however, were hidden away among the hills and not many
people could be seen. There were huge herds of cattle and
droves of goats. The whole country had the appearance of
peace and plenty. There were places which would make
delightful sites for mission stations, and the people, when
found, did not seem to be averse to their settling among
them.

Here, then, Scott decided to establish the first station of
the A.I.M. He found the British Sub-Commissioner very
helpful. The African Elders, while expressing willingness
to have work opened in their midst, were reluctant to let
him have the place he chose, and long palavers were necessary before they would agree.

The site was at an altitude of about 4,000 feet and some
250 miles from the coast. During the daytime it was hot,
as the tropical sun poured down; but at night the temperature sank to the forties Fahrenheit.

The little band of missionaries, with the help of such
Africans as they could employ, set to work to erect a
mud-and-wattle house. When the last bundle of grass was
tied on the roof, Peter left for the coast to bring up the
rest of the party. The journey which had taken them a
month, was completed in nine days by Scott alone! When
he reached the ladies, he found that one of them had
to return to America. When this had been arranged, he
started out with the remainder of the party on 3rd February 1896. They had a caravan of 110 men, and faced
the usual problems as they travelled into the interior but
eventually reached Nzawi on 28th February. By that time

a comfortable brick house was almost completed, and could be occupied. At last the party was reunited in the work they had come so far to undertake. God had met their needs and protected them in their way.

But all seven workers were not needed to man one station. So Peter set out on 11th March to find other sites. Before he did so, he gathered the party together and celebrated the Lord's Supper—the first time they had observed it unitedly since their arrival.

In addition to his other skills, Scott was adept at juggling, tumbling and balancing sticks and knives in different ways. When the Africans refused to give him a suitable site for another station, he won their hearts by giving a display. Before long they gave him permission to occupy the place he had chosen and brought him presents of foodstuffs. So a second station, Kilungu, was opened.

From thence he set out to find a site for yet a third.

By this time a second party of missionaries was on its way. It included Mr. and Mrs. John Scott, the parents of Peter and Margaret. Ina, a younger sister, was also with them. So the family found themselves together once more —in Africa.

Scott was always looking forward, and with the arrival of the new recruits, he saw the possibility of further expansion. At Kangundo some 70 miles north of Nzawi, a military house which was no longer needed was offered to the Mission at a modest rent. It is still one of the central stations of the A.I.M.

Peter Scott's First Annual Report to the Council of the Mission, which was to prove his last also, begins on a note of rejoicing.

'My heart is filled with wonder, love and praise, as I sit down and review the past year of our labours in this

Top left: The Rev. Peter Cameron Scott, Founder of Africa Inland Mission.

Left: The Rev. Lee H. Downing.

Below left: The Rev. R. T. Davis, D.D., American Home Secretary and General Director 1955–1962.

Top right: The Rev. C. E. Hurlburt, General Director 1897–1925.

Right: The Rev. John Stauffacher.

Below right: The Rev. A. E. Barnett.

Left: A pygmy village in Congo. The men are preparing to go on a hunt with their nets.

Below: Playing gospel recordings to a group of Africans at a shopping centre.

land, to which God, by His grace, hath called us. We went out "not knowing", but our God led us forth by a "right way", and brought us to "a city of habitation".'

In the course of his report, Scott made a special point of expressing his gratitude to many officials and members of other missionary societies who, in various ways, had given help and advice.

He recounts the opening of four stations, of bricks made and houses built; of elementary school work commenced with scholars from various parts of the continent; of simple medical work which was greatly appreciated and of steady progress in the language.

He continues:

'And now a word might be said about the people. The WAKAMBA occupy the territory known as UKAMBA, which extends from Tsaro River (this should probably be Tsavo River, Ed.) to Kikuyu. The population is estimated to be between four and five hundred thousand. The men (a great many of them) are naked, with the exception of the brass wire, which is freely worn about their necks, arms, waists and legs. They also make very fine chains out of fine brass wire, and great bunches of these are worn in the ears. They are generally well-built fellows, tall, thin, but muscular. As a rule, they have straight-cut features, are high in the forehead, and rather intelligent in appearance.

'The custom of the women is rather picturesque. In front they wear a small apron of cloth, or goat skin, about five inches long by seven in breadth. Behind they wear a long V-shaped piece of hide, which reaches to the knees, being split up the centre; they also wear an oval hide fastened over the shoulder reaching to the hips. The women do not wear so much brass wire, but the quantity of beads some of them carry around their waists and necks is really wonderful. They are an agricultural people, possessing large herds of cattle and goats. Their manner of cultivation is decidedly crude, as their only implement is a long stick sharpened at the end, with which they turn over the soil, clear the ground, and plant the seed. It is remarkable how much ground they can dig up in a day with one of these sticks. Some few have short-handled hoes, but these are not native. Their tool chest is made up of a very few things and not hard to carry around: a small axe with blade from one-and-a-half to two inches broad, and handle two feet long; then comes a small adze, blade one inch long and handle two feet long; a pair of pincers and a knife. Their weapons of defence are chiefly the bow and arrow, and a long sword. Their houses are small conical grass huts, with a door so small that it is with difficulty you can crawl in when down on all fours.'

Since first leaving Mombasa, Scott had walked 2,600 miles. In it all he had seen the good hand of the Lord upon him and was filled with praise.

This intrepid leader was not spared long for the work of the Mission. He had made a long and tiring journey of 45 miles in one day from Machakos to Nzawi. Shortly after, he began to suffer from vomiting and severe pain. This continued intermittently for about three weeks. When he felt somewhat better, he would rise and continue his work. He had plans to visit Kangundo to see the work there. After that he had in mind to go to America on Mission business. But he became increasingly weak and unable to carry on, and the symptoms of the dread haematuria became evident.

Peter would not allow his mother out of his sight. She

remained at his side, comforting him with passages from the Scriptures. At five o'clock in the afternoon of 4th December 1896 Peter Cameron Scott passed into the presence of the One he had served so wholeheartedly. The last entry in his diary is:

> 'Can we whose souls are lighted
> With wisdom from on high,
> Can we, to men benighted,
> The Lamp of Life deny?
> Here am I, Lord, use me in life or in death.'

One of the missionaries asked Peter whether he had any last words he would like written. His reply was:
'No, not *write*, but *engrave* them:

' "Redeeming the time because the days are evil." '

When it was realized that he might not recover, word had been sent to Kangundo calling for his father and sister. They arrived to see the fellow-missionaries preparing a coffin. It was made from boxes which they covered with white muslin and decorated with flowers.

The following day he was laid to rest in front of the little thatched house in which he had lived.

Thus came to its earthly close a life dedicated to the Master's service. Judged by human measurements it was short. But its influence continued, and the widespread work of the A.I.M. today, and that of the churches which have stemmed from it, is the fruit of that one life laid at the feet of the Lord.

What was the secret of such great usefulness in so short a life? One who served with him in West Africa wrote:

'Near Vungu station was a great tree with roots protruding from the ground, sprawling around like huge legs. Not only had a path been worn to the tree, but a place on a root was smoothed from much use. Peter frequently used it as a seat. There was his trysting place, his prayer chamber, where he read what God said to him in His Book before telling the Lord what was on his own heart. His life story might have come to an abrupt ending in failure when he left Congo had it not been for his intimacy with the Lord in that secret place of stored-up prayer.'

Scott was a remarkable missionary leader, not so much because of his intellectual force, or by reason of great physical vigour, but because of a keen spiritual vision and an ardent missionary heart.

Peter Scott's remains were later removed from Nzawi to Nairobi by his parents.

3

The Darkest Hour

FOLLOWING the homecall of its leader, the young Mission passed through deep waters. A work had been started which, in the purposes of God, was destined to bear much fruit in East and Central Africa. It is not to be wondered at that the Enemy did all he could to stop it. Mrs. Brodie, the friend who had been such a help to Peter Cameron Scott in his hour of need, and who was a faithful prayer-helper of the Mission to the day of her death, referred to the Mission as 'Benoni—Son of my sorrow'.

One after another, several of its valuable workers passed away. Others had to give up for health reasons. Still others—including the remaining members of the Scott family—left to serve Africa in other ways. Margaret Scott married Mr. Wilson, one of the original party, and they settled in the Machakos area.

Eventually Willis Hotchkiss was the only one left. He suffered from repeated bouts of malaria. Food was scarce, and the Africans were hostile and refused to sell to him. For two months on end he had nothing to eat but beans and sour milk. Then came a day when the last bean was finished.

The Africans had agreed that anyone found bringing him food should be put to death. The situation was desperate, but God did not fail. An old woman was in the habit of passing his house as she went to and from her garden. As she harvested her produce she carried it home in a large basket on her back, suspended by a strap around her forehead. One day a root of manioc dropped from her basket as she was passing. The hungry man collected it, presuming that it had fallen accidentally. A day or two later another fell in the same spot. So he watched her. To his surprise he saw that as she passed his house she jerked her head backward, knocking a root off her basket, and went on her way.

Thus the Lord supplied his need through this woman as He employed the ravens to meet Elijah's need.

Later the lone missionary was joined by William C. Bangert. But soon after, Mr. Hotchkiss resigned in order to start a mission for the Society of Friends of which he was a member, so that Mr. Bangert was left alone. Those were formidable days. The rains failed, and famine struck the land. On every hand people were dying of starvation. Mr. Bangert did what he could, gathering a few together on Kangundo station and supplying them with food. But the general situation was heart-rending.

In addition to the famine, tribal warfare broke out. In a letter Bangert said:

'The Wakikuyu are raising havoc again with the Wakamba, drowning all they can get hold of. They have no mercy on women or children; they all fare alike. The Wakamba are fleeing the country and coming back here in large numbers, but it is only a case of "out of the frying-pan into the fire" as they come back here only to starve. . . . Many are dying between here and there, and I have even seen them in trees, *dead*, where they had climbed for the night, to escape being eaten by beasts. Awful is this, but nevertheless true. My heart is wrung and sometimes I feel dazed as I see so much of it.'

At the end of August 1899 the solitary representative of the Mission wrote:

'Sometimes I get a little lonely, and the yearning for Christian fellowship is strong, but after all, I would not have the past two months, in which I have not seen a white face, or spoken in our native tongue, different if I could; because in them I have learned MUCH of and from Himself. In one sense they have been weeks of trial and testing, in another of *great* blessing. . . . The work is large and heavy, and I am nearly played out. It would, of course, be the joy of my heart to welcome a dozen or more, but if the Lord in His wisdom sees fit to withhold any great number, send those for whom He has provided, if it's *only one*.'

A little later he was able to write:

'At last, after almost three months of waiting alone, the glad message has come announcing the departure of two new labourers for this needy field. It is needless to try to tell you how rejoiced I am over the news and I pray that they may become a mighty power for God and good in this dark sin-cursed land.'

Mr. Bangert went to the coast to meet the newcomers, Elmer Bartholomew and C. F. Johnston. By this time a certain length of railway was in existence. Although Machakos is only about 275 miles from Mombasa, the train took three days to cover the distance. Nevertheless, it was a great improvement on safari.

C. F. Johnston was to give thirty-six years to the A.I.M.

and become one of the stalwarts of the Mission. The greater part of his time was served at Machakos. He was a man of God, held in the highest esteem by all. He did not aspire to leadership, but was a strong character and had splendid ideas. At one time he went to work beside Mr. Hurlburt, another strong character. An African woman who knew them both said, in typically native fashion, 'It won't work! If you put two roosters together, will they live in peace?'

After spending a few months with the new arrivals, initiating them into the language and missionary work in general, Bangert left for furlough in March 1900.

The committee which represented the Mission in America met together to seek counsel of the Lord concerning its future. Dr. Arthur T. Pierson, the great missionary statesman, was among their number. After considering the experiences through which the young Mission had passed, he gave his considered opinion, that it had not met with greater difficulty or hindrance than any other Mission that had sought to be wholly used of God; that the difficulties arose from Satanic opposition, and that the Mission ought to go forward. Only as those to whom the testing came laid hold of God's promises in mighty faith would He be able to bless in opening up the Dark Continent to His marvellous light. His advice greatly encouraged those who had made themselves responsible for the work. Mr. Hurlburt, who was already President of the Philadelphia Missionary Council which had stood behind the Mission, was unanimously appointed General Director. Before long he went to the field in company with Mr. Bangert and spent two months carefully studying the situation.

They arrived when the activities of the man-eating lions of Tsavo (described by Mr. Patterson, a railway engineer, in his book *The Man-eaters of Tsavo*) were at their worst. Such scenes have never been paralleled before or since. Mr. Hurlburt wrote of a visit to Mr. Patterson's camp:

'He showed us a boma or thorn fence enclosure where the workmen stay at night to protect themselves from beasts and where only three days before a lion had watched till the first man came out in the morning and had pounced on him dragging him across the railroad track and about fifty feet in the bush where the lioness had joined him and they together had eaten him with the natives screaming and shouting at them less than one hundred feet away.'

Mr. Hurlburt returned to America with a great burden for Africa's people.

He felt that he should reside on the field. The long-cherished desire to go overseas as a missionary was at last fulfilled when, with a party of new workers, he left for Africa in October 1901.

To the surprise of everyone, Mr. Hurlburt decided that his wife and their five children should go with him. It was an act of faith and courage to take them to the Africa of those days. The Lord honoured the step, and in due course each of the five children became missionaries of the Africa Inland Mission. Mr. Hurlburt's example has been followed by many others since that time. This has contributed largely to the happiness of missionary families, and has provided an illustration of Christian home and family life more eloquent than words.

At the time of their outgoing, Mr. Hurlburt wrote:

'God heard our cry and without any appeal save to Him, opened the way for us to go. In this God, with innumerable signs of answered prayer, confirmed the word which He had spoken to our hearts. In no case have we put confidence in a man or human method and found aught but utter disappointment. Every step and every inch has been gained through prayer alone; first, the house on the field was provided for, then with nothing left, prayer was made for the passage money; with this assured we asked for needed equipment and from day to day the need was met. The specific answers to prayer which were beyond the possibility of human connivance would require a considerable volume for their rehearsal.'

The arrival of Mr. Hurlburt and his party in Africa brought new life and expectancy.

4

The Chosen Man

LET us take a closer look at this man who was destined to have such a large part in shaping the Africa Inland Mission and determining its course.

The train drew slowly into Nairobi station as if exhausted by its long tedious journey from the coast. Two young Englishmen stepped nervously from it, wondering what the missionary life on which they had embarked was really like. A tall gaunt figure strode towards them, and, throwing his long arms around them, welcomed them to the field and commended them to the Lord. It was typical of C. E. Hurlburt and won their hearts, as his fatherly way captured the affections of all the missionary family.

'Bwana', as he was known by all the missionaries, had had a humble start in life. He was born at Dubuque, Iowa, on 11th June 1860. He grew up in Oberlin, Ohio, attended school there, and with others of the family, joined the First Congregational Church.

When he was but a lad, his father died, leaving the mother with three sons and a daughter. They had no means of support. Charles, being the eldest, did his best to provide for them, working at farms or factories.

The experiences of those early years induced the sympathy which characterized him.

He learned to lean upon God from childhood. As a schoolboy, the solution to a mathematical problem, which had defied all his efforts for days, was given when he sought it in prayer.

On another occasion the Lord intervened in a way which made an impression on him to the end of his life. It was the depth of winter and all around was deep snow. His mother and he were living alone then. The time came when they had reached the end of their fuel and there was none left for the next day. Together they knelt and prayed, committing themselves and their need to God and asking His help. He was impressed by his mother's quiet confidence, although he could not share it. When they awoke in the morning they were amazed to see a huge pile of wood heaped in the snow outside the house. Together they thanked God for the provision. Some weeks later they met a farmer from a neighbouring town and he asked them if they had been glad of the wood he had left one snowy night. He told them that he had had this load of wood over and above his own needs and remembered Widow Hurlburt and thought she might be glad of it. It had been hard work getting through the snow and when he had reached the house it was in darkness and they were obviously in bed. He decided not to disturb them, but unloaded the wood in the thick snow which deadened all sound, and then went home.

In after years Mr. Hurlburt told of these early experiences of answered prayer, and said what a help and encouragement they had been to him when he was called of God to step out in faith and lead the work of the Africa Inland Mission.

While he was still a youth, the desire to be a missionary came to him. He wanted to take training with this in view; but the door was tightly slammed before him. This depressed him, but as he prayed about it, a strong impression came to him without any unusual or ecstatic experience:

'I have a work for thee to do which thou knowest not of.'

He was giving all his spare time to work for the Y.M.C.A., but he could not feel that this was what the Lord had in view.

Shortly afterwards, the opportunity came to enter full-time into the service of the Y.M.C.A. He welcomed it. The plumbing business he had started, and which had been so successful, he gave to his brother. This entailed no small financial sacrifice, but he took the step in faith, believing that the Lord would supply all he needed. By this time he was married, and had a wife to support as well as himself.

Nor did the Lord fail him. At one time he found that he was unwittingly in debt to his grocer and had nothing with which to pay. He called upon God, and was reminded of the text in Philippians 4: 19:

'My God shall supply all your need.'

A special meeting of the Directors decided just at that time to increase his salary, as from four months earlier. This sufficed to cover the debt and to leave a small balance.

The work he was doing seemed so full of opportunity that he turned to the Lord again and asked:

'Is not this the work Thou hast for me to do?'

But with increased clearness the reply came that this was not his life's work.

As still larger opportunities and responsibilities opened up before him, Mr. Hurlburt asked the same question again and again; but the answer was always the same.

Finally, in 1889, he was asked to become State Secretary

of the Y.M.C.A. for Pennsylvania. This brought opportunities so vast that he felt that nothing could be greater. He therefore gave some days to private prayer that he might be certain whether this was the work that God had for him. But stronger than any previous impression came the word:

'I have a work for thee to do which thou knowest not of.'

A few months later, at a little prayer meeting which was held daily in his house, friends were praying earnestly that God would open the way for Peter Cameron Scott to go to Africa. He needed a committee to stand behind him and the Mission which was being founded, to forward funds and such other workers as the Lord might call. As they knelt in prayer the impression came with the clearest conviction:

'*This* is the work that I have for thee.'

From that time forward he had no doubts but that God had been preparing him through the years for the work of the Africa Inland Mission.

Bwana Hurlburt, while different from the founder of the Mission, was well fitted for work on the foreign field. His resourcefulness was amazing. He could apply mind and hand to almost any emergency, and accomplish most tasks with complete mastery. In those days, when qualified men were scarce in that part of the world, his abilities were put to full use. As a dentist he was ready to help the missionaries and a host of appreciative officials and settlers also.

Ernest Grimwood, who was General Secretary of the British Council of the A.I.M. from 1919 to 1931, says:

'How he loved home comforts after the primitive conditions and fatigue of his African travels; how he loved little children and the simple things of life, with which simplicities may be linked the sublimity of addressing the largest conventions in America, Canada and Britain.

'How he loved the Word of God. On his first journey to Africa he took with him 1,000 volumes, being a deep thinker and omnivorous reader, but when he went on safari, he took one book only—Dr. Arthur S. Way's translation of the Epistles of Paul and the Hebrews. In that remarkable book, "deep called unto deep" as there was so much in the missionary passion of St. Paul that found its counterpart in the unswerving devotion and unstinted labours of Mr. Hurlburt.'

C. E. Hurlburt was a most dynamic character, and at the same time most affectionate. In the early days there was a rapid influx of new missionaries. Most of these were young, inexperienced and sometimes foolish. Yet he was most understanding. Every night he would make the rounds of the missionaries on the station and say 'Good night' to them.

He was a true spiritual father to them all. They all loved him and went to him with their problems. He gave helpful advice, and at the same time sought to lead them more intimately to the One Who had solved so many of his own difficulties.

Mr. Hurlburt laid great stress on prayer, and right from the beginning held a prayer meeting daily and insisted that all should attend.

The then superintendent of the Moody Bible Institute visited Kijabe in the course of a world tour of missions. Of Mr. Hurlburt, he wrote:

'I feel constrained to say that I have never seen any missionary superior to him in all-round, unselfish, capable missionary work. . . . He loves more, gives more and does more than anyone knows anything about.

'I would not forget to include his loving wife for all that has been said of him is true of her also and her daily responsibilities are very constant and arduous.'

The eyes of this man of God were always fixed beyond the horizon, ever looking ahead. He was quick to judge the merits of any particular policy. A lively discussion ranged from the earliest days until comparatively recent ones as to whether it was right for the Africa Inland Mission to engage in anything more than the most elementary form of education. Bwana, however, with his keen discernment said to a candidate who was destined to play a foremost part—albeit in face of much criticism—in the development of education in Congo, that if the Mission could bring the schools to a standard equal or beyond anything that the State could ask for, we could always be in a position to keep them for their evangelistic and other values. This was vision, far in advance of the time, and that of many on the fields too.

As a missionary speaker, Mr. Hurlburt was different from most. Writes one:

'With eager anticipation we waited to hear of Africa's customs, tribal systems, and be given a statistical survey of the vast areas which Mr. Hurlburt was to represent. Instead we were brought into close touch with the Lord of the Harvest. We heard the beat of His loving heart for the lost; our eyes were uplifted to see "fields white unto harvest" and the appeal was for labourers who counted not their lives dear unto themselves, and who had entered into fellowship with Him

Above: Scott Theological College, Machakos, Kenya.

Below: The Opening of an A.I.M. secondary school in Kenya. The Assistant Minister of Education is speaking.

Overleaf: Church and a famous tree at Machakos, Kenya.

Who said, "Other sheep I have which are not of this fold: them also I must bring." '

It was a favourite illustration of his, whenever he spoke of the work of the Mission to liken it to the fingers of a man's hand. The palm rested on Kenya. The thumb pointed towards Tanganyika; the forefinger to Congo; the second on to Lake Chad; the others to Uganda and Sudan.

PART TWO

KENYA
A Fruitful Field

5

Moving Forward

HOWEVER great a leader be, he is dependent to a great extent on others who can share responsibility with him. Mr. Hurlburt was not lacking such.

One of those who accompanied him to the field in 1901 was Lee Downing, a gracious and gifted fellow-worker. He had been on the staff of the Pennsylvania Bible Institute and married one of the students.

Lee was slight of frame and not physically strong. Some of his friends were very concerned when they heard that he was going out to Africa under a 'Faith' Mission which did not guarantee the support of its missionaries. But he waited on the Lord daily that he might know His will, and felt convinced that he was following the right course. This was confirmed when the doctor, after examination, passed him for service in Africa. His long years on the field and the impress he made on missionaries and Africans show that he did not misunderstand the leading.

Things were at their lowest ebb when Mr. Hurlburt went out. Mr. Downing worked with him, and together they brought about the renaissance of the Africa Inland Mission. New life became manifest, showing itself in growth and fruit.

Few people could play second fiddle to a man like Mr. Hurlburt. Lee Downing was sufficiently humble and gracious to do this excellently. Mr. Hurlburt was often on the move, making pioneering safaris, or trips to America or elsewhere in the interests of the work. During his absence, Downing took his place as leader. For many years he served ably as Field Director of Kenya.

Lee Downing had a prodigious memory. He could recite large portions of the New Testament by heart, as well as extracts from other writings which had impressed him. In later years he often spoke at the Kenya Keswick Convention. He did not preach but spoke in a conversational style, quoting freely from the Scriptures. His conversation was not essentially different from his public ministry; both were filled with quotations from the Book he loved so well and studied so constantly.

Prayer had a very large place in his life. He had a hut in a secluded spot where he waited on the Lord daily for the needs of the Mission and the missionaries. There he came to discern the will of the Lord for him. There he received the Divine anointing which made him such a channel of blessing.

I first met the great man in September 1927. He was the special speaker at our Congo Missionary Conference that year. We were mostly young missionaries, and we felt it a great privilege to have such an experienced saint of God in our midst. As he opened up the Scriptures daily, we found ourselves feeding on rich spiritual food. We were encouraged to dig more deeply into the Word to find nourishment for our souls.

But it was not so much the expositions which stand out in my memory, precious as they were. After one of the services, he proposed that we should take a walk together. As we communed together of the things of God, and as, out of his long experience he talked of the Lord's ways, my heart burned within me. That walk and others made a lasting impression on me. It was not my privilege to meet him often; but whenever our paths crossed, I took full advantage of the opportunity of listening to him as he talked of the Lord.

It was this sort of thing which so endeared him to his fellow-workers. He had that all-too-rare gift of godly conversation. Many Africans who went out as teacher-evangelists were affected for time and eternity by his life and influence.

The railway from the coast to Kisumu on Lake Victoria was completed in 1901. In view of the fact that Kangundo, the early headquarters station of the Mission, was not on the route, Mr. Hurlburt transferred the main centre to Kijabe in 1903. Kijabe is about 35 miles north-west of Nairobi and stands on the slopes of a range of thickly wooded hills. The railway then passed within 2 miles of the mission station. It has since been realigned and traverses a part of the land which was originally given to the Mission. The line now passes close to the two-storey house which was occupied for many years by the Downing family.

From the mission station there is a clear view for many miles across the Kedong Valley, out of which Longonot, an extinct volcano, with a crater some 800 feet deep and 2 miles across, stands as a landmark.

It was intended by Mr. Hurlburt that new missionaries arriving on the field should spend a period at this healthy station, learning something of the language of the area in which they were to work and getting adjusted to the conditions of their future service. Kijabe station is at an altitude of approximately 7,500 feet above sea-level. It stands amid a forest of cedar and wild olive trees. The streams, coming from high up in the hills, gush down with a plentiful supply of cool fresh water. Being so high, Kijabe can be very cold and mosquitoes do not breed there. The name means 'Place of Winds' because of the breezes which blow there constantly. The soil is very fertile and European vegetables grow there all the year round. Rainfall is heavy at certain seasons and at those times the roads become seas of slippery mud.

A young American who was to share with Bwana Hurlburt much of the pioneering of the early days arrived at Kijabe in 1903. He was John Stauffacher, a surname which has been on the list of missionaries from that day to this. John was of Swiss extraction. His godly parents were dairy farmers in Wisconsin.

But not for him a farmer's life. He and a like-minded cousin were students and read every book of a serious nature they could lay hands on. The first two dollars they earned were spent on books by Livingstone and Stanley, and together they prayed that God would send them to Africa. For this they did all they could to prepare themselves. They 'lived rough', blazing trails. John gained as much knowledge as he could about farming, and also learned to cook. He delighted in nature and was fond of music and art.

Accepted by the Mission, he sailed in 1903, but not before he had become engaged to Florence Minch, a teacher.

Arriving in East Africa, he wrote:

'On the afternoon of August 26th, I found myself on one of the trains of the Uganda Railway, speeding on toward Inland Africa. Had you been standing on a little foot-path on one of the mountains near Kijabe, and watched the train as it passed along, you would have seen at one of the car windows, a face half hopeful and half anxious. . . . The train had not yet reached Kijabe and I was anxious because we were rapidly passing by some of the most beautiful scenery I had ever seen. . . .

In a few minutes we arrived at Kijabe. . . . I soon noticed, however, that a man was anxiously looking for someone, and that someone turned out to be myself. In a few minutes more I found myself hastening back to the very same foot-path on the mountain side which I referred to. The path goes winding up a very steep hill, a hill which one never forgets when once he has climbed it. After stopping several times, we came to a small opening, and before us stood a grass house, the then headquarters of the Mission. This, at last, was the end of a long journey over land and sea. . . . After a few rounds of handshaking and hearty greetings, there came around the corner of the house the "famous mule".

'It seems impossible for one to spend a half-hour at the station without at least climbing on the mule's back. So we started off across a short stretch of level land to the spot where the permanent buildings are to be located; they are now nearing completion. . . . There I got my first glimpse of the Kikuyu people. In a moment there was wild excitement. Then there came a grand round of handshaking and greeting such as only these natives can give.

'After these greetings were over, we began to look around for objects of interest. We were delighted to see the familiar tall and straight old cedars; we also noticed the branching wild-olive, and many trees strange to our eyes. Back of us towered the high hills, while before us stretched an immense plain, the feeding grounds of thousands of Masai cattle, and, we hope, the grounds which shall witness a great triumph of the Gospel among the heathen.

'The view from the location of the permanent buildings is just grand. The wooded hills circling about, the great plains before us, with the volcanic mountains, Longonot on the one side and Suave on the other. The hills back of us are covered with immense gardens, cared for by the Kikuyu people. We have plenty of timber for building purposes. Within half a mile of the station are several fine mountain streams, giving us an abundance of clear fresh water. Heat is almost unknown here, the nights especially being very cool. Sickness is very rare and fevers are unknown. We are within two miles of the railroad station (considerably less, since the line was rerouted) thus giving us the facilities of the homeland. Have we not many reasons to praise our God for His goodness in providing such a place from which to extend the kingdom of His Son among the fallen races of Africa?'

John was appointed to work among the Masai—a nomadic people who, at that time, lived near Kijabe. Later the Government moved them farther off. This tribe owns large herds of cattle and the people constantly move from one place to another seeking pasture. The assignment appealed to him and he looked forward to the day when he could take it up.

But before he was ready to do that, he must be introduced to missionary work and learn something of the language so that he could speak to the people. Like many another missionary he soon found himself engaged on tasks which were unexpected. He took charge of the dispensary, giving simple remedies and applying dressings and bandages. He learned to build a mud-and-wattle house, to make bricks and burn them in a kiln and to teach the nationals to do these things. The Africans, who are so adept at reading character, took quickly to the tall missionary, with his dark hair and complexion. They appreciated his graciousness and enjoyed his fun. He was one who easily made friends, whether among white or black.

He longed to go and settle among the Masai, but they

were hard and difficult. They were fierce warriors and stories of the atrocities they committed made many afraid of them. John gave much time to prayer, asking the Lord to open the way to reach these people and in answer the miracle came about. One day as he and others were working in the forest two African men arrived, bringing a woman. She had a running sore on her face and they asked for the big doctor to treat her. Although he had no medical qualifications, John washed out the sore and bandaged it. He was overjoyed when he discovered that they were Masai, feeling that by this means the way was being opened into their country. The sore healed quickly.

As a result of this, a friendship sprang up. The local Masai elders sent some young fellows to help John learn their language and invited him to visit them in their village. He had other providential help too. Mr. Holler, the first Secretary of the East Africa Protectorate, had made a study of the language and the tribe. When he heard that John was going to work among them, he sent him all his notes.

Before long John was able to move freely among the tribe, although two years earlier a white man would not have been allowed to live for two hours; for the Masai were dangerous people and many had warned John that he needed to be on his guard.

Eight months elapsed, however, before he was given permission to settle among them. By this time the Government had moved the tribe some 60 miles farther away, and John went to live at Laikipia.

John's fiancée arrived in January 1906. They were married in the following May. Meanwhile John had suffered from recurring attacks of malaria and had to return to Kijabe where he could have better care. Even there he was so ill that right up to the day of his wedding he had to spend the greater part of his time in bed. He could only attend the church by being taken there in an ox-cart and carried on the back of a fellow-missionary into the service during which he sat on a chair. The newly-weds were not able to set out for their site at Laikipia until nearly a month later. They travelled part of the way by train, but they had two days walking to do before reaching their destination.

The one to whom John was thus united was a true help-meet. Of the six children of her Christian parents, three became foreign missionaries.

Life was difficult for a missionary wife and mother. She had to make tiring safaris from time to time, in addition to facing the difficult climatic conditions and hardships of other kinds. Malaria often laid her husband low. Frequently she was left alone with her children. But she rejoiced in it for the Gospel's sake. She did all she could to bring the Masai to Christ. Classes were commenced to teach them to read and write, and to give them instruction in Bible truths.

Those who knew the couple in after years realized that John would never have been the man he became were it not for the woman God gave him. He hated hypocrisy and sham of all kinds, and this led to an appearance of being boorish or even uncouth at times. Many ordinary amenities seemed to him to be unnecessary and to savour of sham; and he would not tolerate them. He would some-times express himself candidly and without much tact when missionaries were discussing their work, and this gave rise to difficult situations. But it was all part of his honest integrity, and both Africans and missionaries loved him for this quality. Florence, however, by her winsome ways and friendly nature was a great help to him, and was often able to smooth out misunderstandings.

John Stauffacher, like P. C. Scott, C. E. Hurlburt, Lee Downing and many others, was a man of prayer. At

Kijabe he could be seen making his way to a little stream in a deep ravine about a quarter of a mile from the houses. Here amid the cedar and olive trees, the wild flowers and ferns, he read his Bible in quietness and communed with God. Surrounded by the beauties of nature which he loved, his solitude often disturbed by the troops of chattering monkeys or baboons, he would meditate and pray and study. Later, at Laikipia, he built a house in a tree to which he could repair for the same purpose. Wherever he was, he maintained a place of prayer. There, like so many others, he found his strength and spiritual power. That was the secret which led to so many miracles of God's intervention and blessing.

So the work went steadily forward. By the end of 1906 the missionary force numbered thirty-one. They occupied seven stations. Apart from the one opened by John Stauffacher among the Masai, all were in the Akamba and Kikuyu country.

With Lee Downing to look after the routine running of the work, Bwana Hurlburt was able to make a number of safaris, looking for openings among other tribes as yet unreached. Many hazards were faced in the course of these, and many were the experiences of God's protection and overruling.

Early in 1907 the Bwana and John made a long trip to the north-east among the Samburu and Rendille tribes. It was unknown country, semi-desert. As they went on, the land was increasingly dry and hot, and the low thorn bushes tore their clothing to shreds.

Wild animals abounded, including rhinoceros, giraffe, zebra and various kinds of gazelle. The travellers camped beside the Uaso Nyiro River for the weekend. Fish could be caught so easily that they soon tired of the sport.

The Samburu people welcomed them and gave them

presents of sheep and goats. Some of the people showed great interest in the Gospel and asked significant questions.

From there they went farther north towards the area occupied by the Rendille tribe. They understood that this part of their safari would not take long, so they decided to leave most of their goods behind, and take merely a blanket each and a little rice. At night they made a stockade of thornbush and slept under the stars. But they found it was farther than they expected, and there was very little water to be had. Either it was found in very muddy holes, or in deep wells. From these the cattle were watered much as in Bible times. Men stood at intervals on the sides of the well, and the waterpot was handed from man to man and then poured into a trough.

After six days of overpowering heat and longing for fresh, clean water, they came in sight of palm trees. Here they reached different country. There were no more cattle, but hundreds of camels. Things had not seemed strange to them among the Samburu, for they resembled the Masai; but everything was different in Rendille country. The appearance of the people and their customs surprised them. Even their huts were different, a framework of poles covered with hides and mats made from the fibre of a kind of cactus.

The people received them kindly and gave them camel's milk to drink and camel meat to eat. When the camels were brought to the village for the night, they made a loud groaning, like the slow creaking of heavy machinery. This noise was so loud that, when the people offered them one of their huts to sleep in, they felt that they must decline, or they would get no rest. So, finding a place near a well whose water they could drink, they spent the night there.

From there they set off through strange country without a guide. For the first two days they found water and good places to sleep, although the only food they had was a little rice. Supposing that they would still find water, they did not carry any with them. They had expected to reach the river at the end of one day's safari; but they were mistaken. However, seeing green trees in the distance, John and his Akamba companion hurried on in front of the rest. As they approached the place, their way was blocked by a rhinoceros. They shouted at it, and eventually the beast condescended to move away.

When they reached the trees, they were encouraged by finding a series of wells. But the first four they examined were dry. John hurried on to a fifth; but, with a savage growl, a lion started up almost at his side. He had no weapon, and made for the nearest tree. But the lion made no attempt to follow him, so he hurried back to the rest of the party to get his gun. They hesitated to attack the beast; but their situation was desperate, and there was nothing else to do. So they approached it with three guns. Mr. Hurlburt and he fired simultaneously, and with their second shots, the beast fell dead.

But still they found no water. They pulled the lion's carcase out of the pit, and then, discouraged and disheartened, they lay down and went to sleep. At midnight they were awakened by a rhinoceros which snorted near by, but caused no trouble. Then again, intense thirst wakened them. They decided to go down one of the wells and try to find water by digging. By morning they had collected just enough to make tea; but it was brackish and seemed to increase their thirst.

It was the Lord's Day, but they dared not remain there. They pushed on as soon as it was light in an endeavour to reach the river. All were suffering intensely from thirst by now, and had eaten nothing for twenty-four hours. It was with the greatest difficulty that they persuaded the Africans to continue.

Before long they descried more palm trees in the distance and felt certain that it must be the river. John and his companion, Mulungit, rushed on. But Mulungit's mouth was so parched that he could hardly speak and his strength soon gave out. John hurried on alone, and when he reached the palm trees he felt that he could not go a single step farther. All he had found was a bed of dry sand.

He sat there, his head swimming. After a while, he regained his strength and prayed as he had never prayed before. What should he do? If he went back, the men would refuse to go another step. If he went on alone, he might be lost from the party, and nobody knew where water could be found. Yet he must do something. It was no use sitting still.

As he sat there, the Lord drew very near.

'Had I seen the Lord beside me,' wrote Mr. Stauffacher, 'I could not have been more sure of His presence. I was sure He would guide me to water.'

He pulled himself together and struggled on. He crossed three more river-beds, but found no water. A fourth one was in sight.

Desperately he forced his unwilling feet towards it, tormented by the thought that even there he might not obtain the precious liquid. His temples burned like fire; his lips were so parched that he could hardly part them.

As he drew near, he caught sight of a man in front of him. It was Mulungit whom he had left by the way when his strength gave out.

And there at last was the river. They were saved. Without stopping for anything, John plunged in, clothes and all, and buried himself in the waters. Mulungit staggered and could not reach the stream. However, when he had had a drink, and water poured over him, he revived a little.

Leaving him sitting beside the waters, the missionary started back to find the remainder of the party. His clothes were heavy with water and he was weak. He discarded some of his garments and started again. He rushed on through the thorny brush, shouting as he went. In a little while he heard a rifle shot, and thus found his way to them. Mr. Hurlburt had been urging the men on. They were strong young fellows; but the General Director was the strongest of the lot.

The men crowded round, and the water he brought was shared among them. With new courage they hurried on until they reached the river. The difficulties and perils were soon forgotten as they rejoiced in the supply of water. In their desperation they had eaten no food for two days; but it was not long before a meal was prepared, and they found new strength.

They rested a day by the river, and then followed it towards their camp.

As if they had not yet had enough excitement, another rhinoceros attacked them. It tossed the mule, injuring one of its legs, and almost caught John too; but he managed to dodge behind a tree as the great animal lowered its head to charge.

The camp was farther off than they had imagined, and it was after dark when, shedding tears of gratitude, they were welcomed back. They sat down to a rich repast of hot rolls and coffee, of jam and milk and sugar. Luxury indeed, after the shortages of the past fifteen days! They rejoiced over the Lord's protection and praising Him for His care, they soon fell asleep.

After that, they hurried home. It meant crossing flooded rivers; but they were so anxious to meet the ones they had left behind that they did a double-length journey the last day.

They had been away for exactly four weeks and had travelled about 400 miles.

Political and other restrictions made it impossible

to establish work among the Rendille people for many years.

Another stalwart joined the ranks of the pioneers at the end of 1907, introducing a name which has ever since appeared more frequently than any others on the A.I.M. roster.

Albert Edward Barnett was an Australian who had gone to America to study flour-milling. There he heard the call to whole-time service for the Lord. After training at Moody Bible Institute, he went to Africa in a party of twenty-three led by the Lee Downings returning after their first furlough. They arrived at Mombasa on 3rd December 1907, and eventually reached Kijabe by train about nine o'clock the following night. Bwana Hurlburt and others were on the platform to welcome them.

On arrival at the Mission they were shown into a long house built of bamboo poles and mud, divided into several rooms. They welcomed it. The train journey had been hard and tiring, and soon they were fast asleep in comfortable beds. But it did not last long. Thousands of black pinching ants invaded the house and they had to rise to disperse the aggressors with hot ashes. They succeeded after a long struggle and were able to settle down in their beds again. What an introduction to life in the wilds!

After spending a few weeks at Kijabe, Mr. Barnett joined Mr. Hurlburt and several others to prospect for new stations. They found suitable places among two tribes, one at Kilombe, the other at Kapropita. A. E. Barnett was left to open work at the former site among a branch of the Masai people.

A little later he married Miss Nicher, a nurse and masseuse from Sweden who had also trained in America. Together they entered enthusiastically into the work.

But they were not at Kilombe for long. When the Stauffachers were leaving for furlough, the Barnetts were asked to go to Rumuruti. Mrs. Barnett was no stranger to the station and its people. She had lived there before her marriage.

When the Stauffachers returned after furlough they were given other work. Papa and Mama Barnett (as they were called by all) remained at Rumuruti for four years until they, in their turn, went on their first furlough.

On their return in 1913 they went to their former station of Kilombe which had been without missionaries since they had left it. The house which Papa Barnett had built was still standing and habitable. But their growing family meant that more accommodation was needed; so he set to work to erect a larger dwelling. Miss Slater who had been a fellow-worker at Rumuruti was also stationed at Kilombe.

On one occasion the whole congregation consisted of one young woman. Mama talked with her, telling her how the Samaritan woman met the Saviour at Jacob's well. As the message was pressed home, she responded and had personal dealings with the Lord Jesus Christ that day and entered into new life, the first Masai woman of those parts to come to Christ. She developed into a bright Christian and many of her relatives turned to the Lord through her testimony.

She came to live near the station. One night when the Barnetts were asleep, their house caught fire. This woman was the first to observe it and rushed to waken them—an act which they felt saved their lives.

In the meantime, an independent work was started among the Luo. It was later integrated into the A.I.M. In 1906 Mr. and Mrs. Innes and Miss Boldt, who had all worked among the Zulus in South Africa, heard of the need in East Africa and started pioneer work at

Ogada, on the hills to the north of Kisumu, overlooking that town and Lake Victoria. A half-caste Zulu girl came with them and was a great help as they set about mastering the Luo tongue.

Their first convert was a man who interpreted for Mr. Innes as he preached. He was baptized and took the name of Johana. Later he became chief in his district and maintained a consistent testimony until his death in 1931.

Nyakach, to the south of Kisumu, was opened in 1911. The work prospered and expanded rapidly. From the beginning indigenous principles were introduced and in time evangelists, teachers and pastors were raised up.

Mr. and Mrs. Innes continued in the work in East Africa until both were past their eightieth birthdays. Later years were spent at Kericho, where they carried on an evangelistic and pastoral work among the people who flocked to the town and surrounding tea plantations in search of employment. In his last year, Mr. Innes rejoiced to see the erection of a church building there.

Not until 1913 was it possible to open a station in the Kamasia tribe. It was at Kapropita on a range of hills dividing the Rift Valley. Mr. and Mrs. A. M. Andersen were the missionaries. He had left his native Denmark for America where he was soundly converted. Going to East Africa, he worked for a while in the industrial mission started by Mr. Hotchkiss. Here he met and married Miss Vivian Waldron, and they joined the A.I.M. The industrial work he developed at Kijabe was so fruitful that it was with the greatest reluctance that their request to engage in pioneer work was granted. But the move was of God, and they were used to open no less than six stations, one of them Kapropita. After a few years, however, this had to be closed. In 1926 a station was opened in the same tribe at Kabartonjo; but as the work grew, its facilities proved inadequate. Subsequently the centre was transferred to another site at Kapropita.

The Andersens also opened Litein among the Kipsigis people, and here the last eleven years of Mr. Andersen's life were spent. Andersens of the third generation are now numbered among A.I.M. missionaries.

6

The Kikuyu Controversy

A CONFERENCE in 1913 in which Mr. Hurlburt played a leading part, aroused extensive interest. It was concerned with missionary co-operation in East Africa. As the Gospel was preached, young churches were produced. It seemed tragic that the denominational differences which divided Christians in the homelands should be imported into Kenya. The Kikuyu Conference, and the smaller gatherings which had preceded it, was constituted to investigate the possibilities of closer fellowship between the churches. The four main Missions then at work in East Africa were represented. Mr. Hurlburt had been one of the leaders in formulating the proposals brought before the Conference.

The basis of fellowship which was passed by the Conference included the loyal acceptance of the Holy Scriptures as the supreme rule of faith and practice, and of the Apostles' and Nicene Creeds; and in particular the belief in the absolute authority of Holy Scripture as the Word of God, in the deity of Jesus Christ and in the atoning death of our Lord as the ground of forgiveness.

What was proposed was not organic unity but federation which would bind the different Missions in a closer fellowship.

At the close of the conference a united communion service was held, led by the Bishop of Mombasa.

The conference, although concerned solely with the local situation, provoked widespread reactions. The Bishop of Zanzibar wrote a strong letter of protest to the Archbishop of Canterbury asking for an enquiry into the proceedings, followed by another indicting the Bishops of Mombasa and Uganda for heresy. The Archbishop placed the matter before the Central Consultative Body of the Lambeth Conference. The war then intervened, and it was not until 1915 that the Archbishop made his pronouncement on the Kikuyu controversy. While he took a sympathetic attitude to the Conference, his reply was cautious, and counselled against members of Anglican churches taking communion at the hands of those not episcopally ordained, or the holding of united communion services.

A further conference was held at Kikuyu in 1918. The same bodies were represented, and the Bishop of Zanzibar, the Rev. Dr. F. Weston and a representative of the Universities Mission to Central Africa were present by invitation. Bishop Weston put forward his own proposals for a united church, but these were unacceptable to the other parties.

The formation of a united church was thus found to be impossible and the most that could be done was in the form of an Alliance with a basis similar to that proposed for the Federation.

Later the Alliance High School came into being at Kikuyu. This was governed by its own Board, on which the Alliance, the Government and others were represented. Its staff was appointed by the Board but approved by the Representative Council of the Alliance.

In 1924 the Kenya Missionary Council was formed to represent all Protestant missionary work. At first membership was confined to missionaries, but later Africans were admitted and others interested in or associated with missionary work. This subsequently became the Christian

Council of Kenya, on which both churches and missionary societies have representation.

Later attempts at church union have been made, but neither the Africa Inland Mission nor (more recently) the Africa Inland Church have felt free to associate with them since they involved the compromise of essential principles.

7

The First World War and its Aftermath

THE outbreak of war in 1914 had many repercussions which affected the Mission and its missionaries. Many British subjects were called up for military service. In addition a large 'Carrier Corps' was conscripted from Africans, and many leading Christians were enlisted. A band of Christian men was organized, led by missionaries. These included Dr. Kenneth Allen, Mr. Alexander, Mr. Stephenson, Mr. J. Guilding and Mr. Albert Clarke of the A.I.M. Dr. John Arthur of the Church of Scotland Mission led the group. Regular services were held for the men, as well as catechism classes. The spiritual health of the Christians was maintained, and, although they had to face hardships, they retained their happy spirit, and had many opportunities of witnessing to the truth and power of the Gospel. The Government recognized their value and the Acting Governor of British East Africa referred to the 'Kikuyu Missions Volunteers' in a speech he made to the War Council at Nairobi, in the course of which he said :

'A carrier section of 1750 mission "boys" was formed, officered entirely by members of the missions' staffs with Dr. Arthur in command. A number of the older mission "boys"—men who in many cases were far over military age—joined up as headmen. I recently had the privilege of inspecting this unit at Kikuyu shortly before it left for the front and was greatly struck with the general appearance of confidence and efficiency.'

Among those who thus volunteered to act as headmen were several outstanding men. One of them was Mulungit. He was the son of a wealthy Masai chief. Converted in early life by hearing the Gospel from a passing missionary, he went to Kijabe and became Mr. Stauffacher's right-hand man. He had to endure considerable persecution from his clan and tribe, and even the Government was for a time unwilling that he should give up his position as prospective chief to live on a mission station. Mulungit himself passed through a very critical time of fierce temptation, but eventually he came through to victory. He and Mr. Stauffacher became staunch friends. Evening after evening they would sit together translating the Scriptures into the Masai language. They went on safari together, Mulungit's previous travels having taught him the way through large parts of East Africa. When the Stauffachers went on furlough in 1909 the way opened for Mulungit to go with them and to have further education in America. He stayed there until 1912. On his return he proved very useful in the work, getting on well with both Africans and Europeans.

Another of the volunteers was Tagi. When the Stauffachers opened work at Laikipia, they erected their mud huts on a site which was not far from a government fort. The troops for the fort were recruited from the African population in the surrounding district. A happy acquaintance sprang up between the missionaries and the officers, and in May 1908 the latter gave permission for one of the government buildings to be used for Sunday services for the troops. Among those who came was a tall, slender sergeant. This was Tagi.

It was not long before Tagi, in learning to read, realized that he was a sinner and needed a Saviour. When he received the Lord Jesus Christ, he yielded himself to Him in entire devotion. This gave him new incentive in his studies and in less than four months he was able to read both in Swahili and Masai.

As he learned more of the things of God, a deep longing possessed him to pass on the blessing to others. Although he was offered promotion in the army with a considerable increase of pay, he gave up his career in order to devote himself to the preaching of the Gospel. This step was taken in the face of much opposition. He had a gift for languages and before long he had mastered English and used an English Bible in his own private devotions. He could translate direct into Masai or Kikuyu with the greatest fluency, while reading the English text.

He was offered an opportunity of going to America for further studies, but decided to remain at his post since the missionaries from the Laikipia station were going on furlough, and he could hold the fort.

Having been brought safely through the hazards of war service, he continued his work as a preacher of the Gospel. He translated the whole of the New Testament into the Masai language. Previously only the Gospel of Mark had been available.

His life of usefulness was cut short, however. One evening he did not return home. When search was made for him the next morning, he was found dead. It was suggested that the trigger of his rifle had caught in the firewood he was gathering and the bullet had pierced his heart. His unexpected passing was a great grief to missionaries and Africans alike.

John Guilding, one of the British missionaries who went with the Carrier Corps, had come out to the field in 1913.

He and Mr. R. B. Flyn had worked together in a caravan with the Children's Special Service Mission in Great Britain. They both applied to the A.I.M. and came out to the field together. Their destination was Congo, but owing to lack of funds they were held up in Kenya. So they worked at Nyakach among the Luo under the kindly supervision of Mr. Innes.

It was not until January 1916 that they were able to proceed to Congo. Working together at Bafuka, they came into great personal blessing. But Mr. Guilding could not feel that Congo was the Lord's place for him, and at the end of the year he returned to Kenya.

Then it was that he was called up for military service. He was released a year later, by which time German East Africa had been cleared of German troops.

During the war years missionaries continued to go forth both from Europe and America. But they were not exempt from the usual hazards which warfare presents. The S.S. *City of Athens* on which many missionaries were travelling, including nineteen of the A.I.M., struck a mine in August 1917 as the ship was nearing Cape Town. In the mercy of God all of the party were rescued, although some narrowly escaped drowning when one of the boats capsized. Fifteen missionaries of other societies and four of the crew lost their lives. The people of Cape Town welcomed the rescued party and rushed to supply their needs. In spite of the terrifying experiences they could testify to the Lord's goodness and faithfulness. One of their fellow-passengers, a Jew, professed conversion, and when they landed, confessed his faith in Christ without fear.

Nor did the war prevent the expansion of the work. In 1914 Mr. and Mrs. Propst opened work among the Nandi tribe at a place called Aldai. The C.M.S. had commenced a station in the tribe as far back as 1908, but had abandoned it after three years. The station at Aldai was subsequently closed in favour of Kapsabet, where Mr. and Mrs. W. Mundy carried on the work.

The 1920s brought a severe crisis in the church in Kenya. It arose over the question of female circumcision. This is a custom which is followed by the Kikuyu and a number of other tribes in East Africa. About the age of puberty, the girl is taken to a camp in the forest, and given instruction in behaviour and tribal custom. The operation is then performed by certain of the older women, without anaesthesia or regard for asepsis. It is accompanied by heathen rites. Serious complications often occur at the time of childbirth due to the scars which this operation leaves.

For long the missionaries realized that this custom was inconsistent with a Christian profession, but its hold on the whole population was such that nothing could be done about it. It was believed, almost universally, that the girl who was not thus mutilated could never bear children. Christian girls who were prepared to take a stand against it were few, and invariably they were seized by their parents and forced to submit to the rite.

At last the missionaries and church elders felt that a definite stand should be taken against the practice. The decision provoked a violent reaction. The Kikuyu Central Association, a political body, opposed it vehemently, saying that the church by condemning polygamy and female circumcision was destroying African culture. These customs were made a test of loyalty to the Association, who told their adherents that 'they must destroy the church at once', if they hoped to preserve their rights. Severe persecutions arose. Christians were abused and threatened with death. Mission schools were placed under a boycott. Blasphemous utterances were flung at the missionaries and vile, indecent, wholly indescribable dances were engaged in. At mission schools, teachers and pupils were subjected to indignities and to a continual fire of insulting epithets. Christians maintained their position at the risk of their lives. Many fell away. Other buildings alongside the churches were erected and independent services held in them, or in the open air near by. Many of the meetings were violently anti-Christian, and were used for political propaganda. The elders of the church took a strong line and insisted that all church members sign a statement to say that they did not agree with female circumcision. Few were prepared to take this step and many left the church. On one occasion, the only people to partake of Communion in the Kijabe church were five elders.

Feelings ran high. In January 1930 one of the lady missionaries at Kijabe was murdered. She was killed and mutilated in her own house. Miss Hulda Stumpf had come to the field in 1907. Her previous business experience proved extremely useful at Mission headquarters both when it was at Kijabe and when later it was transferred to Congo. But she returned to Kijabe. She was a deeply spiritual woman, loved by all. With the other missionaries and church leaders she had taken a stand against the degrading practices, and it was generally felt—although never proved—that it was this which led to her death.

The first to see Miss Stumpf's body was one of the elders who has since taken a leading part in church life in Kenya —Mr. Andrew Wambari Gichuha.

Slowly the church recovered from its setback. Members who had fallen away because of the high standards adopted, gradually found their way back, and numbers built up again. But the standards were never relaxed and those who returned had to accept them.

8

Expansion between the Wars

AT Kapsabet, the Mundys were followed by Rev. and Mrs. Stuart M. Bryson, a couple who had been converted in adult life while they were farming in New South Wales, Australia. Hearing the Lord's call to missionary service, they sold their farm to take up training. Bwana Hurlburt visited Australia about that time, and through his ministry they were led to Africa. They arrived in 1919. For the first two and a half years they worked at Kijabe and learned both Swahili and Kikuyu. They were then asked to go to Nyakach to take charge of the work there, relieving the Inneses who needed furlough. John Guilding was also stationed there. Since they were now among the Luo people, they set to work to learn another language. John had worked there previously and already knew Luo.

In 1927, after furlough, the Brysons took over the work among the Nandi. Once again they had to learn a new language. A few Europeans had dabbled in it and the Gospel of Matthew and the Epistle to the Romans had been translated; but nothing in the form of grammar or vocabulary existed. So the Brysons set to work to learn the language from the people themselves. They collected Nandi words on pieces of paper and stored them in a biscuit tin.

They realized that if the Christians were to be established they must have the Bible in their own tongue. As soon as they had enough of the language, they set about the task of translation. God had prepared a helper for them. Samuel Gimnyigei had been converted as a lad and in due course had become an evangelist and teacher. He was intelligent, and Mrs. Bryson taught him English in the hope that he might eventually help them in translation. The church leaders agreed to his doing this work. It cost him a lot, however, for it involved leaving his outschool and his wife and children each Monday morning, spending the week at Kapsabet, returning home only at weekends. For years on end he did this, assisting in the translation of the whole Bible. It was published by the British and Foreign Bible Society in 1939. The translation was thus the work of Stuart Bryson and the Rev. Samuel Gimnyigei (he has been ordained since those days) with help from Mrs. Leftley (then Miss Frances Collier) and Mr. Reuben Lagat.

The Nandi Bible is used by a group of interrelated tribes numbering about 185,000. The Kipsigis, however, were not happy in the use of this translation, since there were certain marked differences of dialect and words between it and their own language. In view of this the translation has since been revised by Miss Frances Mumford, assisted by Mr. Ezekiel Birech and others. The union language is now known as Kalenjin.

The Brysons worked among the Nandi until 1938, when Mrs. Bryson's health necessitated their retirement in Australia. Stuart then became Secretary of the A.I.M. Committee in that country. This became a full Council of the Mission in 1961.

A number of other tribes of this group had had to be by-passed in the early years, and it was not until 1931 that it was possible to advance into their territory. Rev. and Mrs. Reynolds were the leaders.

They were an outstanding couple, beloved by both

Europeans and Africans. Reg had been born in Australia, but while he was an infant his parents moved to South Africa. There he had his education. A trip to East Africa with his father, herding cattle and hunting, brought him into contact with missionaries. A casual remark made by one of them made him conscious of a great lack in his own life, and led eventually to his conversion. He went to the Moody Bible Institute in Chicago, and, after graduating, he married a Canadian fellow-student. He often said that he had been born in Australia, brought up in South Africa, trained in America, married in Canada, worked in Kenya and his citizenship was in Heaven!

They arrived in Kenya in 1925. Their first few years were spent at Githumu, one of the older Kikuyu stations. Reg became an expert in Swahili, taking advanced government examinations.

Later, Reg was asked to make a survey trip into the tribes to the north of the township of Eldoret. This entailed travelling over 2,000 miles by car into territory occupied by the Marakwet, Geyo, Tuken and East Suk (Pokot) tribes. In some parts there were no roads at all. On the floor of the Rift Valley, in the low burning plains of the Pokot they had to cross unbridged rivers, as well as river-beds where water was only seen at the height of the annual rainy season.

During the course of this long safari they visited places which had never before been reached by missionaries, and where the Gospel was unknown. Only those who have seen the precipitous hills and deep valleys can appreciate all that this and subsequent safaris cost in physical endurance. As a result of these journeys, the whole area was thrown open to the Gospel.

While out on the Marakwet Escarpment with Rev. A. M. Andersen and Mr. Harry Lunn, a group of tribesmen gathered. One of them expressed his concern about God's death. He said that several years previously God had died and, although He recovered later, things had gone wrong since then. The locusts had come and devoured their gardens, for one thing.

The missionaries were puzzled. But after some conversation they linked the occasion with an eclipse which had occurred at that time. The people there worship 'Asis' (the sun) and they had interpreted the eclipse as the death of their deity. The conversation that ensued led to the request for an evangelist to settle in their midst to tell of the true God, the One who created the sun, the moon (the sun's wife), the stars, the earth and all people, and whose Son had indeed died for their salvation.

In 1934, following the safari, it was proposed to open a station at Kapsowar on the Marakwet Hills. A small government centre had been evacuated and the Mission sought permission to take it over. Response was favourable, especially as the opening of a medical work was promised. Much local opposition was shown, however. One Somali, who owned a nearby shop, fearing the moral effect of Gospel preaching, swore that no missionaries should live there while he was alive. Within three days he was dead! This shocked the local inhabitants. Opposition was withdrawn, and the missionaries moved in. At first Reg himself lived there and supervised the opening of the work; but when the Brysons went home, he made his centre at Kapsabet. Apart from furloughs, the Reynolds remained at Kapsabet until, in 1959, Reg was made Acting Field Director during the furlough of Rev. Erik Barnett. This necessitated his removal to Nairobi.

Kapsowar commands one of the most magnificent views of any station in the Mission. It looks across the great Rift Valley to hills on the opposite side. There is a drop of about 4,000 feet to the floor of the valley, where the air is hot and the earth arid. Beyond that there is a correspondingly high escarpment, and Kapropita stands above it. On the hills the climate is pleasant and the nights cold.

The whole countryside consists of steep hills with deep valleys between them. The villages are perched on the hillsides, and the stamina of an athlete is required for village visitation. These conditions do not seem to trouble the Marakwet themselves, however. Old men and women climb the steep slopes with no apparent difficulty, while young warriors, responding to the 'wagat' (distress call) trot up them, brandishing their spears and knives, bells tinkling on their ankles.

There is an interesting system of irrigation throughout the Marakwet country. The waters of the Kerio River are tapped high up in the hills and, by means of channels winding round the slopes, the gardens throughout the tribe are supplied, each section in turn being watered at different times of the day.

Harold and Marjorie Powley went to Congo in 1924. After serving at Bafuka among the Azande people until 1936, they were advised on medical grounds not to return to those parts, and so transferred to Kenya. This was a sad loss for the Congo work, for they had learnt the Azande language and had won their way to the hearts of the people.

They reached Kenya in time to take charge of the work at Kapsowar when Reg moved to Kapsabet. Marjorie Powley has 'green thumbs', and delighted in the fertile soil on the station. But they were only there a short time. When the Second World War broke out in 1939 Harold was called up for military service, and Marjorie went to live at Nairobi to be with him. She taught in a government school there.

A couple of young doctors—Leigh and Marion Ashton —were loaned by the South Africa General Mission to open the medical work.

When the Powleys left the writer and his wife transferred from Congo and went to Kapsowar. We were very
happy in the work, but only spent two and a half years
there. In the meantime, Leigh Ashton joined the
forces, Marion found the altitude too much for her and
moved to Nairobi. The nurse who had worked with them
was invalided home, and we were alone with Miss Margaret Halliday, the Girls' Worker.

The development of the Marakwet work was slow, and
the people unresponsive. The initiation rites, when boys
and girls are circumcised, had a firm hold on the people
and made an effective barrier to the Gospel.

With the arrival in 1944 of Dr. and Mrs. W. B. Young,
the work made better progress. Bill was a Cambridge
Rugby Blue and a Scottish International. He was just the
man for tramping up and down the Marakwet Hills. He
mastered their language in record time and quickly gained
the confidence of the people. But his wife's health necessitated their leaving the field after only a few years. Dr.
Philip Morris—son of Fred and Madge Morris, pioneer
missionaries in Congo and West Nile—served there for a
while.

One of the earliest difficulties concerned the supply of
water. Kapsowar being on a hill and the river far below
in the valley presented a problem. A firm of hydraulic
engineers was consulted, but they advised that it would be
impossible to pump water to such a height at such an
angle. Dr. Jim Propst from Kijabe had a look at it and
produced a scheme by which it could be done. While plans
have had to be modified to overcome various difficulties
which have arisen in practice, there is now a good water
supply from the river.

When the work was first started, a boy was employed
to chop firewood for the hospital. He is now the senior
dresser and an elder of the church.

The doctor usually had to be Station Superintendent as well as running the hospital. Occasionally there were others available to assist, but invariably the exigencies of the work and the shortage of personnel meant that they had to be sent elsewhere. Margaret Halliday married Mr. Herbert Hanson Young and they were there for some years.

Dr. Stanley Lindsay went there in 1953, and apart from furloughs has remained ever since. He married one of the nurses—Pauline Driskell—and together they have given a spiritual lead to the work. There has been considerable development in the medical department as well as in other directions.

In answer to prayer and in miraculous ways, money has been provided for the building of additional wards, the purchase of an X-ray plant, a generator to supply electricity and for the erection of buildings to house these. A providential combination of circumstances made it possible to procure a new X-ray table at half-price.

In the course of his voyage back to the field in 1930 Reg Reynolds led to the Lord a young South African student—Tom Collins. Called to missionary service in East Africa, he was later used to open up the Suk (now called Pokot) tribe to the Gospel, as well as to initiate work among the Turkana.

His life was one long struggle against ill-health. Rheumatic fever when young had left him with a seriously damaged heart. On this account he was rejected by the Mission when he first applied. But the call of the Lord was such that he went out at his own expense. He tramped out among the Suk tribesmen in the semi-desert country in the north of Kenya. He gained an excellent knowledge of their language, and was already a master of Kalenjin. To these he later added Kiswahili and Turkana. He translated parts of the Bible into the Suk language.

By this time the Mission had accepted him into membership, in spite of his physical condition. During his many safaris in the Suk country he faced almost incredible hardships, footslogging most of the way, spending the nights in native huts, under the stars or even in trees. His iron will and passionate devotion to the One Who had saved him overcame his physical handicap as far as possible, and his selflessness led him to hide his condition from others.

He married Ruth Barnett and together they opened mission stations at Kinyang and Liter.*

Many others there have been whose lives and labours are well worthy of inclusion in this record. They have left behind them a rich fragrance. The McKendricks, the Farnsworths, the Kenneth Allens, Dr. Blakeslee, the Teasdales and others did noble work. But space does not allow of it.

The Masai cannot forget the Shaffers. Roy Shaffer came to Christ in his youth. While still a young man he was appointed a 'circuit preacher' by his church. Thus began the nomadic career which was to find its culmination in thirty-five years of safari in East Africa.

Roy and his wife were assigned to work with the John Stauffachers among the Masai. They travelled the 65 miles to Siyapei in a two-wheeled mule-cart. Almost the whole of their missionary career was spent among that tribe, which they learned to love and admire. They saw many lives transformed through the preaching of the Gospel. A boy called Kuyoni, the eighth son of a local witch-doctor, became a Christian, in spite of persecution from his father. He was cursed and disinherited. Yet he persisted and later the witch-doctor turned to Christ. Kuyoni was readmitted to the family and given his father's blessing.

*The full story is told in *Tom Collins of Kenya* by K. N. Phillips (Africa Inland Mission).

A few years after they had come to live at Siyabei the Shaffers employed Kuyoni, now a teenager, as a cook. He attended school, and worked for them in his spare time. A good scholar and a faithful servant, he was baptized and took the name of Peter. Called to the ministry, he entered the Bible School at Kijabe and graduated in 1933. When he married a Christian girl after graduation, his was the first Christian wedding on Siyabei station.

During an evangelistic safari which the Shaffers made, a Masai chief heard the message and invited them to open work at Loitokitok. Peter and his new wife went with them as fellow-workers. They were the main helpers when the first school for Masai girls was opened at Lasit. Today, Peter is an ordained pastor.

Loitokitok was only one of many places where the Shaffers opened work. Three of these are now mission stations, most of the others are school or church centres.

They left the field in 1958. Two celebrations in widely separated parts of the tribe were arranged in their honour. With tribal ceremony and speeches, presentations were made to them. Roy was given a 'sceptre of authority' made of rhino horn. Only twice before had such a sceptre been presented to a white man. Roy was given two—one at each celebration.

He was not the only missionary to receive such honour from Africans.

In 1960 Reg Reynolds was found to be suffering from leukaemia. This necessitated his retirement to South Africa. When the elders of the Nandi church heard that he was leaving the country they decided to give him a 'Sambut'. This is a fur coat made from monkeys' skins. These are sewn together and lined. This kind of cloak is only worn by very important Nandi elders and then only on ceremonial occasions. Nandi priests wear them when praying for rain or for victory over their enemies. This

was an honour only given to two other Europeans—
Princess Margaret and a Chief Native Commissioner.

In South Africa, Reg led the South African Committee
of the A.I.M. and built up the work there. For four
valuable years the disease was held at bay, but he succumbed to it towards the end of 1964.

Reg was never satisfied with anything less than the
best. Every house and path had to be exactly in line. The
Africans, so apt at giving nicknames, called him 'Kiptober',
the Straight One—straight, not only in outward matters
but also honest as the day.

A favourite illustration of his, which made a strong
appeal to the Africans, was that of a team of oxen. The
whole team must pull together if progress is to be made.
If one animal pulls towards another direction, the cart will
not go forward.

As a photographer and cinematographist, Reg strove
for perfection. He would never show anything less than
the best, and some of his films rank with those of the
highest professionals.

9

Problems of the Second World War

WHEN the Second World War broke out, work in Kenya, Tanzania, Congo, Uganda and Central Africa was already well established. The Sudan advance had not yet been commenced. A few of the missionaries were called up for military service. Others offered themselves as chaplains. Tom Collins joined the medical corps, as did Ken Phillips. War service by no means brought their Christian work to a standstill, rather it increased their opportunities. Ken Phillips later became a chaplain to the forces, both European and African. These served in Ethiopia and Kenya. Welles Devitt also became a chaplain and went to Burma with the East African forces, returning with a decoration in recognition of his distinguished services which went far beyond the usual duties of a chaplain. Harold Powley became a Captain in the East African army.

In Congo, Fred Lasse took up duties as a Protestant Chaplain with the Congolese forces.

Travel by sea was difficult and perilous during the war years. An Egyptian vessel, the S.S. *Zamzam*, sailed from America in April 1941 with two hundred civilian passengers on board. About one hundred and sixty of them were missionaries and their children of various societies. The A.I.M. party consisted of nineteen adults and seven children. Conditions on board were very insanitary. When within a few days of Cape Town the ship was intercepted by a German raider and shelled. The lifeboats were destroyed and the vessel badly damaged. The passengers were transferred to a prison ship and spent five weeks dodging the British blockade before reaching occupied France. Since the United States was not yet involved in the war the Americans were repatriated, but three who held British nationality were interned. They were John Guilding and his wife and William Mundy. Mrs. Guilding, a Canadian, was released about a year later, after having passed through many distressing experiences.

Mr. Guilding and Mr. Mundy had to spend three years in various internment camps, undergoing at times considerable hardship before the latter was released on health grounds in August 1944. John Guilding was detained until relieved by allied forces the following April. These had witnessed a bold confession wherever they had gone. Mr. Guilding conducted services and gave Bible Readings, leading a number to the Lord. He was invited during the course of his detention to take part in escape plans; but he declined, assured that the Lord had placed him there, and that when the right time came, God would arrange for his release.

When eventually he was freed, he was able to visit his aged father, his sister and her family in England before going on to Kenya to rejoin his wife. Both the Mundys and the Guildings gave further valuable service to Kenya.

The life work of John Guilding and his wife was in the Bible School at Machakos. This was conducted in the local vernacular, and during the course of their years there large numbers of Akamba were trained as evangelists. The whole tribe owes much to their faithful ministry and to the grounding in the Word of God given to them.

The years of war were destined to have a great influence

on Africa. Although the full extent of this was by no means foreseen, wisdom was given to the Mission, and measures adopted forestalled much trouble. In Kenya, the churches which had been formed as converts gathered in groups were linked together as the Africa Inland Church. This move gave Africans an increasingly larger part in church affairs, and led to a deepening and expansion of the work of the Lord.

But in Africa as a whole, the war introduced a time of much unrest. Many national troops went overseas, acquitting themselves well. They fought beside European soldiers in Egypt, Burma and other countries. On their return they were not prepared to settle down to tribal life again. They had had their eyes opened. The demand for self-government became clamant, together with the return of lands occupied by Europeans.

The Mau-Mau rising in Kenya came out of this. It took the form of opposition to everything European and all that they had brought—including Christianity. It was a continuation and an intensification of the earlier methods of the Kikuyu Association. The whole of the Kikuyu tribe was swept into it, and other tribes were affected also.

People were rounded up in their villages and, after being instructed and warned by oath-administrators, were forced to swear oaths involving secrecy, obedience to the leaders of the society, even to the extent of murder. Many of them were anti-God, anti-Bible, anti-Mission as well as anti-European.

A certain number of nominal Christians fell away, but almost all the members of the Africa Inland Church took a stand against the movement. Many who refused to take the oaths were ill-treated or martyred. A highly respected Christian chief was shot while travelling in his car. Another chief, attempting to break up a Mau-Mau gathering, was hacked to pieces. Some of the Christians

made very courageous stands, witnessing to their mur-
derers even when at the point of death. Almost one
thousand Christians lost their lives.

Barbed-wire entanglements were erected around the
missionary houses in the affected area, and military guards
posted at strategic points. A home guard of missionaries
and African Christians numbering about one hundred and
forty men co-operated with the soldiers in keeping watch.
More than once the rebels purposed to attack the Mission,
but their plans were frustrated. The names of the church
leaders were high on the black list, but they took an
active part in opposing the movement in spite of this.

In an attempt to eradicate this trouble, many troops
had to be employed for a long time, and some of the
leaders were never caught. But the Government came to
realize that a movement as deep-seated as this could never
be overcome by force of arms alone. What was needed
was a change of heart, although it would never be couched
in such terms officially. The Missions were therefore encouraged to hold services in the concentration camps
where many thousands were detained. The Pocket Testament League visited these camps too and preached the
Gospel among the people, giving away portions of Scripture to those who would take them. Various missionaries
and African Pastors did valuable work among the de-
tainees, and wonderful stories of clear-cut conversions to
Christ were recorded, as a result of which lives and out-
looks were completely changed. Ken Phillips was much
used among them, as was also Pastor Johana Nyenjeri of
Kijabe.

Not only by way of personal contact was the seed sown,
however. The Government also arranged for time to be
given to the Missions in the Broadcasting Programme from
Nairobi. As the Gospel message was given out over the
air, great blessing resulted and many today look back to

the time of detention as one during which their lives were radically transformed.

This led to today's radio ministry in Kenya. The Rev. Robert Davis, son of the Rev. R. T. Davis, General Director of the Mission, took special training with a view to developing this ministry. Gifts were received which made it possible to erect a studio at Kijabe. Here services, musical items, sermons and Bible studies are recorded and broadcast from Nairobi. Theodore Teasdale, another second generation missionary, was skilled in the technical side of electronics and worked with Bob. Together they produced high-quality recordings. An average of ninety minutes daily is given to broadcasting recordings made in the Kijabe studio in a number of African languages and in English, and even more time is expected. Opportunities are also given on television.

Transistor radios are to be found even in the farthest reaches of Africa in these days. The Mission is straining every nerve to make full use of this modern method of preaching the Gospel.

It was a serious blow when Bob Davis passed away in 1965 following a heart operation.

The Lord had His man ready, and Pastor Timothy Kamau is now in charge of the broadcasts.

10

Medical and Other Ministries

FROM the very earliest days in Kenya the missionaries gave medical help. But for the most part it was done at the back door, and often by people who had little or no training along such lines. As time went on, dispensaries were opened, but it was a long time before anything more elaborate was thought of. Dr. Henderson, the earliest doctor, gave valiant service. Dr. Elwood Davis opened a small hospital at Kijabe. After all, there were doctors in private practice in Nairobi—some of them Christian men —to whom the missionaries could go when they were ill, and the Government was opening hospitals in the larger towns and dispensaries in the smaller places.

Later, however, the need for a medical centre for the Mission was realized. A well-equipped hospital was planned for Kijabe. Departments of medicine, surgery, obstetrics and gynaecology, ophthalmology and dentistry were envisaged. Plans were drawn up in faith for a hospital consisting of six blocks and one hundred beds. Only a small proportion of the money needed for the first block was in hand when the first sod was turned in 1959. But the Lord honoured the step, and within eighteen months that building was ready for occupation. Of the other blocks only the maternity department has been erected so far. Some of the required specialist staff were also provided, but the need still exists for many more.

Dr. W. Barnett, a highly trained and painstaking doctor, is in charge and has set a high standard for the hospital. The writer personally and many others owe much to his care and skill.

Dr. Jim Propst is also stationed at Kijabe. His care is that of the station dispensaries throughout Kenya, each of which must be visited at least once a month. He is also a skilful hydraulic engineer. His parents and also his grandmother were missionaries at Kijabe before him. The story of the hospital at Kapsowar has already been told.

When Tom Collins, in the course of his numerous safaris, saw the need of the 160,000 unreached Turkana, he reported it to his superiors. Much prayer was offered that personnel might be forthcoming to open work among that tribe. It was felt that the first approach should be along the medical line.

The Lord was preparing his chosen instrument. A young doctor was concerned to know the Lord's will for his life and became burdened for the needs of the Turkana. Accepted by the Mission, Dick Anderson travelled about that hot sandy country in a jeep, running a mobile clinic and looking for a suitable spot for permanent work. Eventually one was found on the banks of one of the few rivers where a reasonable water supply was available. The place was called Lokori—'The Place of the Giraffe'. Building presented unusual difficulties. The nearest source of supplies was almost 200 miles away, and the roads were atrocious, so that tyres only lasted about 1,500 to 2,000 miles. In spite of all the handicaps, however, missionary residences and a small hospital have been erected.

Although the effort was spearheaded by the Mission, it was actually a co-operative venture between Mission and Church. A Missionary Board had recently been inaugurated, and its first representative went there. Pastor

Peter Mualuko, a Mukamba, was trained at the Machakos Bible School. His first thought was to go to the Southern Sudan; but his application for a residence permit was refused. He then turned his attention to the Turkana tribe. Since going there, Peter and his wife have had to face many trials and testings, but they are still there, and are now at a post deeper in the tribe. A number of schools and evangelistic outposts have been opened at various centres, and another Mission Post has been manned at Kalokol, on the shores of Lake Rudolf. Others are envisaged in other parts of the northern Frontier District. Conditions in this whole area are physically trying. God be praised for those Africans and Europeans who are willing to face them to carry the news of a Saviour's love to those who for so long have sat in darkness. The Lord has encouraged them by giving some who have publicly confessed their faith in Christ.

The Africa Inland Mission and others have received very much help from the Missionary Aviation Fellowship. The inauguration and maintenance of work in this and similar places would be almost impossible without their aid. Their plane, based in Nairobi, is kept busy on behalf of missions, conveying doctors or mission officials to out-of-the-way places, transporting emergency patients to central hospitals, saving not only valuable time but lives also, and ameliorating the lot of those who labour in difficult places. The plane makes the trip to Lokori once a month regularly and more often when needed, carrying fresh vegetables and other commodities. The flight to the nearest centre takes less than an hour each way. When the same journey has to be done by road, fourteen hours of hard driving (not counting delays for punctures or breakdowns) must be endured. I and very many others have been grateful to the M.A.F. when visiting Lokori, Tanzania, the Central African Republic and other places.

More recently another plane has been stationed in North-East Congo to serve the stations reopened after the troubles.

Another agency which has helped immeasurably to spread the Gospel has been the Gospel Recordings. The devoted representatives of this Society go to remote parts of the world and record approved Gospel messages in the languages of many different tribes. These are then put on gramophone discs and sent in large quantities to the parts of the world where the language is used. Cheap gramophones are specially manufactured and supplied at very low cost so that the poorest may obtain them. By this means, the records reach far away places. They are played over and over again to many audiences until they are known by heart and can be repeated verbatim.

There are thousands of Asians in East Africa. The first of these were employed in building the railway. Many stayed on and others followed, supplying the need for craftsmen, or becoming wholesale or retail traders. In order to reach these with the Gospel, International Missions of America has sent missionaries who work in association with the A.I.M. There has not been sufficient of them properly to meet the needs of Kenya, let alone those in Tanzania and Uganda.

The task is difficult. Most of them are tightly bound to their religions, be they Hindu, Sikh, Moslem or other. They are eager for their young people to learn English, and on this account the missionaries are frequently requested to teach that language in Asian schools. This provides opportunity for witness. They are also asked to teach 'The Life of Christ' in some of the high schools.

Libraries of Christian books have been established in several places, and these are very popular. Camps for the young people are proving very profitable spiritually.

The work requires much patience and wisdom. Fruit is

scarce, yet there are encouragements, and faith expects more.

So this fruitful field of Kenya has progressed until now well over half the six hundred missionaries of the A.I.M. are fully occupied in it, and yet only touching the fringes of the opportunities which it affords. Work is centred around some forty stations, with others waiting to be opened. The work ranges from the most primitive contacts with illiterate tribes-people to ministry among the most sophisticated. For some the approach must be on the very lowest level; for others, educated, critical, under the influence of modern trends of thought, the presentation must be on a higher cultural plane. Yet for all, ignorant or lettered, 'The basic trouble is sin,' as an educated Christian African once said in my hearing, 'and the only remedy is the blood of Jesus Christ.' The Gospel message, applied by the Holy Spirit, is effectual to the salvation of all sorts and conditions.

PART THREE

TANZANIA
Sowing beside the Waters

II

The Door Opens

In 1908 Mr. Hurlburt had to take a short furlough in America to deal with business matters for the Mission, and to talk with the Council regarding the new developments. God was in it. Not only did he have many opportunities of making the work known and enlisting further help but in a marked way the Lord brought him into touch with key people who were destined to have an influence on the furtherance of the aims which Peter Cameron Scott had set before the Mission.

Mr. Hurlburt was surprised to be summoned to the White House to meet President Theodore Roosevelt. He wanted advice concerning a hunting holiday he was planning in East Africa. Afterwards he would visit the Belgian Congo. In the course of conversation, the work of the A.I.M. was mentioned and its plans for advance in a north-westerly direction. The President was impressed and interested, but no more was said, and the interview was brought to a close. Seed had been sown, however, which was destined to bear an important harvest.

On his way back to the field, Mr. Hurlburt had as fellow-passenger for part of the voyage, Bishop Tucker of Uganda. They had many conversations together, and the Bishop asked Mr. Hurlburt whether the A.I.M. would be prepared to take over their work in what was then German

East Africa. They had only one station, and that was at Nassa, on the east coast of Lake Victoria. It was difficult to administer it from Uganda, where the rest of their work was situated. Nassa had a history. Work had been commenced there in 1888. When Alexander Mackay had been driven from Uganda, he had found refuge there.

But Mr. Hurlburt hesitated, for it was not in the main direction of their proposed line of stations to Lake Chad. However, when Bishop Tucker invited Bwana Hurlburt and John Stauffacher to see the field, he agreed to go.

Accordingly they set out on 7th January 1909, going by rail to Uganda and then across Lake Victoria. This is the second largest freshwater lake in the world, covering an area of 26,828 square miles. It resembles a sea more than a lake. It can be very rough at times, when dark tropical storms accompanied by gale-force winds break over it. Both the Bwana and John suffered from seasickness on the lake steamer. Ordinarily, however, its waters are placid, and a light breeze plays over them. The surface reflects the colour of the sky—blue in the sunshine, grey on a murky day, almost black when the storm-clouds lower. The sunsets are magnificent, a riot of colour, when sea and sky seem to be ablaze. Sandy shores or wooded slopes border on the lake, and sailing boats tack hither and thither as they skim the waters, conveying passengers or freight from one place to another, or collecting the fish harvested in the traps.

They spent a happy day at Nassa, meeting the missionaries, the African chief and some local Christians. Then they made their way farther south in order to study conditions. At Mwanza, some 60 miles west of Nassa, at the south-eastern corner of the lake, they found a modern port, with European buildings, and streets lined with flamboyant trees. In bygone years it had been an important port for the slave traders. Away from the town, the vil-

lages were much as they had been in the days when
Speke first caught sight of the waters of the lake in 1858.
The huge mango trees planted by the Arabs still stand
there, and Arabs still sit beneath them.

They continued their journey south. Safari, like all
safaris in those days, was tiring and eventful. They soon
left the comforting shade of palms and mango trees, and
the cheerful blossoms of the town. They found the greater
part of the country flat and uninteresting.

Tabora, the inland capital of German East Africa, was
disappointing. Food was scarce and expensive. Most of
the springs were brackish. Mangoes and coconuts grew
in great profusion; but apart from these, all they could
buy was a little dirty rice and some tins of plain water-
biscuits.

The place had attractions, however, for all the pioneers
of early days had passed through it. Livingstone had spent
some time there, and they met an old Arab who had been
employed by Speke on his exploring tours, having letters
of recommendations from him as well as from many others
of the early African explorers and missionaries. He
claimed to have worked several months for Livingstone,
but this could not be substantiated.

A faithful Mukamba lad had volunteered to accompany
them and to serve them on this long safari, but towards
its end he, too, suffered from malaria, and was so weak
that he had to be carried in a chair.

Eventually they reached Mwanza again, and embarked
once more on the lake steamer. At the end of two months
safari, the accommodation, which at other times might
have called forth severe criticism, seemed palatial. Conditions had been hard; but the people had been unusually
friendly and polite. This is still true today and the visitor
is impressed by their good humour.

The Sukuma tribe numbers about one million, and there

are other smaller tribes in the area. Missionaries of the Church Missionary Society had learnt the Kisukuma language from the people, and reduced it to writing and had translated part of the Scriptures. As early as 1895 St. Matthew's Gospel had been printed by the British and Foreign Bible Society, but owing to a series of accidents, only two damaged copies ever reached the Mission. Other portions were printed later. In 1913 the Gospel of John, which had been revised by Mr. Sywulka, one of the early A.I.M. workers, was printed at Nassa on a small hand press. It was in 1944 that the complete New Testament was printed by the British and Foreign Bible Society. The whole Bible was issued by the same Society in 1961.

As a result of their safari, Mr. Hurlburt decided to accept Nassa from the Church Missionary Society and to commence work in that territory. They began to pray for workers. The Stauffachers went on furlough with the vision of the needy people of north-west Tanganyika before their eyes.

12

Prewar Years

THE Rev. and Mrs. Sywulka were sent to Nassa. Emil Sywulka had been born in Austria, but when he was four years old his parents went to America and settled in northern Wisconsin. They were very poor and the children were brought up amid deep poverty and privation. His home was Catholic and at an early age Emil was admitted to the Roman Catholic Church.

He recorded the following before leaving for the field:

'It was shortly after my first confession that the Lord called me to give my life as a missionary to Africa. The Catholics have the habit of praying the Lord's Prayer for anything they need. I used to spend my time, whether at work or while going on errands, in repeating the Lord's Prayer for this that and the other. One day while walking along the railroad track and thus praying, the Lord spoke to me about Africa and I prayed the Lord's Prayer that he might send me there as a missionary. From that time to this it was always my desire to go as a missionary to Africa; to-day that desire is a burning fire.'

In May 1898 Emil definitely yielded his life to Christ. He worked on his father's little farm until he reached the

age of twenty-one, and then began to teach in a school
away from home. Some two years later he came across a
copy of the (American) *Christian Herald* in his boarding-
house.

'I don't know to this day how it got there,' he wrote,
'but the paper contained a description of the Moody
Bible Institute in Chicago. As soon as I read it I said,
"I am going to that school." I believe God Himself sent
that paper into my home. The next fall I went to the
Moody Bible Institute of Chicago and attended it for
three winter terms of eight months each, successively.
Since I had very little money God graciously supplied
my need by giving me something to do. . . . I can truly
say that God has fulfilled Phil. 4. 13 and Phil. 4. 19 in
my life.'

He first arrived on the field in 1906, and was set to
work at Kijabe. In 1907 he married Miss Schneider, a
nurse from Akron, Ohio.

Bwana Hurlburt asked them to take up the work at
Nassa.

Hundreds attended the morning service on the Sunday
following their arrival. But there was a restlessness among
them. They would not settle down. Finally Mr. Wright
said :

'They want to see the baby.'

Few of them had set eyes on a white baby before. The
infant was handed to Mr. Wright who carried it up and
down the aisle that all might see. This satisfied them and
the service was able to proceed.

Within three weeks the Sywulkas were alone at Nassa,
the C.M.S. missionaries having left for their new assignment. Before they left a communion service was held.
Sixty-three Africans partook.

Each Sunday the church was filled with hundreds of people; but before long it was discovered that they came simply because the chief ordered it. When the command was cancelled the large building was nearly empty! And of those who came many were reprobates and incorrigibles.

This situation was discouraging in the extreme. Of this time, Emil Sywulka wrote later:

'Nothing but a God-given courage could have taken us through those days of awful disappointment and trial of faith.'

If the missionaries were dependent on natural resources they might well have given up in despair. But it was God's work, and they looked to Him for the solution. Mr. Sywulka spent long hours of prayer and fasting on the hill behind the station and in other places.

After about two years, their hands were strengthened by the coming of Miss Jacobson. She was a one-talent worker. She was not qualified for preaching or teaching, nor had she administrative ability. Her one gift was that of prayer.

Things began to happen. Attendances improved. People came to Christ. Some were so anxious that they came to Mr. Sywulka's office to ask the way to salvation.

As other workers came, stations were opened at Mwanza, Nera and Chamagasa.

One day two men came to the office and the following conversation took place:

'Teacher, we have read these words and they have convicted us "Beloved, if God so loved us, we ought also to love one another". We are asking you to let us go to take the words of God to others who know Him not. May we go?'

'Brethren, with all my heart I want you to go, but have no money with which to send you.'

'Money! We want no money, only let us go.'

And they went out to preach the wonderful Gospel.

Pioneer work was hard. Although new workers were added to their numbers, some became discouraged and left; others had to be invalided home. Several passed away, one of whom had been less than a month on the field. In spite of serious illness, the Sywulkas continued in the work.

Late in 1912 Emil went to Kijabe, Kenya, to attend a meeting of the Mission Council at which he represented the urgent need for help in German East Africa. As a result of the Council Meeting, Mr. Sywulka was able to return with Mr. and Dr. Maynard, Miss Bowyer, Mr. Green and Mr. Malek. In those days, it was impossible to send advance notice of local travel, and the party arrived at Nassa unheralded. Mrs. Sywulka records the occasion as follows:

'On the afternoon of their arrival at Nassa, we and our African helper were about the King's business in the dispensary, cleaning house and we looked it. Seeing a shadow on the wall we turned towards the door and there stood two ladies, who introduced themselves as Dr. Maynard and Miss Bowyer and also informed us that the rest of the party would be along soon. Our prayers for more labourers were answered. The exercising of sudden unlooked-for, unplanned-for hospitality was rushed upon us—rooms, beds, food. Naturally our thoughts flew kitchen and pantryward. Being alone with two little folks meant that, while we had enough good food, the shelves were not loaded down with a lot of extras. The new supply from Kenya, where all our staple groceries were bought, was on the way. Dr. Maynard, being a housewife, naturally thought how in the world is this crowd to be fed. As always the Lord met the need. It was a rare thing to have a man come with fish late in the afternoon, but that day there he was! About the same time a man appeared with the hind quarters of a buck. Thus, a few hours after their arrival they, as new missionaries, had their first lesson taught them according to Phil. 4. 19 and "Thou preparest a table before me".'

Shortly after, the Maynards and two single ladies left to open the new station of Kola Ndoto. It was 150 miles south of Nassa and they had to make the journey on foot. It took them ten days. On arrival they lived in tents until houses could be built.

Later that year the Sywulkas left for furlough. Owing to the outbreak of war in 1914, ten years elapsed before they were able to return to what by then had become Trustee Territory.

13

The Years of War

IN 1914 there was neither airmail nor radio broadcasts. The missionaries knew nothing of the declaration of war on 4th August.

The Maynards had sent a runner to Mwanza to cash a cheque and to bring mail. His return was delayed, and when he arrived it was with empty hands. No boat had arrived from Kenya that week and there was no mail. Moreover, the bank had refused to cash the cheque as a state of war had been declared between Great Britain and Germany, and no money was coming through from the bank in Nairobi.

At that time there were only seven workers left on the German East Africa field. Some had just left for furlough, some had resigned for other reasons. Of the seven, one couple, being Canadians, were interned by the Germans. At Nassa were Mr. and Mrs. Rudolph Malek, and the Maynards and Miss Bowyer were at Busia (now Kola Ndoto).

These were completely cut off for a long time. In spite of efforts by the American Consul at Zanzibar, no news could be obtained of the isolated missionaries, although there was no reason to doubt their safety.

Those were days of deep experiences for them. It was not long before Mr. Malek, being German, was called for war service and his wife went to join other women in similar circumstances. This left only Mr. and Dr. Maynard and Miss Bowyer on the field. Before long their supplies were exhausted, and the situation seemed impossible—no wheat flour, no sugar, no tea, no white potatoes, no baking powder and other commodities usually regarded as essential to a European household. Can God provide a table in the wilderness? Ensuing experiences demonstrated that He is still the same God as of old, 'absolutely dependable'.

These things had not taken God by surprise and He had His way of providing. The last boat which arrived had brought a rifle and ammunition for Mr. Maynard. He was able to shoot game. This provided meat for their own table. The remainder was bartered for rice, maize flour and other things from the Africans. For twenty-six long months they were cut off from home mail, funds and supplies.

In Shinyanga, some 10 miles away, a German baby was very ill. Dr. Maynard visited the home several times, walking, or being carried in a carrying chair each way. Finally mother and baby came to the mission station so that the Doctor could give better attention. When it seemed that hope must be abandoned, the Lord intervened and gradually the little one returned to health. The grateful father supplied the missionaries with many of the things they so sorely needed but could not buy—fresh vegetables, sugar, tea, etc. So God spread a table for them.

A friendly Greek visited the station from time to time, enjoying the society of the missionaries and in return provided supplies they were unable to purchase.

During the year 1915–16, the little Doctor had three attacks of the terrible blackwater fever. The third of these was particularly severe, and when she sank into a deep coma, neither Mr. Maynard nor Miss Bowyer expected her to recover. However, the Lord restored her, and the severity of the disease passed; but she was very weak. There was no food available except that which they could obtain from the local Africans, and it was coarse and quite unsuitable to tempt the palate of an invalid. Try as they would, it could not be made attractive, and the patient could not swallow it. She was starving to death.

'If only I could have a slice of white bread and a potato, I believe I would recover,' said the Doctor one morning, in extreme weakness.

But such commodities were not to be had. White potatoes did not grow in that part of the country. And as for white flour, none had been obtainable since the beginning of the war in 1914! It was an impossible request. Miss Bowyer, however, asked the Lord to supply them; Mr. Maynard also prayed, but with little faith.

That day was one of gloom and depression for all. Even the Africans sensed it and went about their duties with an air of silent despondency.

'Hodi!' The call at the door was heard late that afternoon. Mr. Maynard went out, wondering what the caller wanted. Standing in front of the house was an African woman, a complete stranger. She handed him a rather bulky parcel. Curious to see what it contained, he took it to the table and opened it. There, to his utter astonishment, was a loaf of white bread and twelve potatoes! He could hardly believe his eyes. God had sent the answer to prayer by the hand of this stranger. She was God's raven!

Before long the sick Doctor was sampling the luxuries. She began to recover at once.

The explanation came the next day. A German officer and an African askari appeared. They were seeking information regarding British military movements, and had sent the parcel in advance to prepare their way. God had provided for His sick child, in answer to prayer.

As Mr. Maynard said at the time:

'The God of Elijah still lives!'

The Doctor quickly regained her strength after this, and before long she was back at her work.

As time passed, the tide of war turned, and the Germans sensed the possibility of defeat in East Africa. A German official in Shinyanga feared that, should the British advance, they might be interned. For himself, he could endure it; but he would spare his wife and child that experience. So he asked the missionaries if they would allow the woman and child to live at the station. Reluctantly they agreed. The Doctor rebelled at the thought of more mouths to feed. A mud-and-wattle hut was built for them, and they took up residence. But the extra mouths to feed proved to be the channel through which they were all fed, for the husband continued to send far more than was needed for his wife and child, and provided the station with much that had been lacking.

In 1916 the fighting came near them. Wounded soldiers, white and black, were brought to the little mission station. Mud-and-wattle huts were hastily erected to house them. These constituted the first hospital the Doctor had had in Africa. Not the white buildings, and screened-in windows and gleaming equipment she had seen in her daydreams; but far better than the little shed in which she had worked hitherto.

Then came the word 'Mwanza has fallen to the British'. It was not long before British troops arrived at Kola Ndoto. All German officials were interned, and the mother and child, who had been given refuge at the Mission, were taken also. The mud-and-wattle house was left vacant. Quickly the Doctor made it into a dispensary. And she could stand erect—the whole 5 feet of her—under every part of its roof!

14

The Postwar Period

THE war was over, but famine supervened. The rains did not come and crops failed. The missionaries suffered. The rifle continued to provide meat which had to be bartered for a little rice, or grain or a scrawny chicken. The wooden floor of the tent, which had originally been used as a dispensary, was cut up and traded for food.

The Africans suffered badly. Many died. Villages were emptied, the living often being too weak to bury the dead. Skeletons could be seen on the paths, hyenas having pounced on the corpses and devoured the flesh. There was no milk to be had; for the cattle too had died.

Disease followed. Those who had survived the famine fell victims to the scourge of influenza. Some managed to crawl to the mud-and-wattle dispensary, but there were not enough medicines left after the war years. Nor could the Government help, for they had no supplies.

Wild animals, also famine stricken, became bolder and bolder. Again and again appeal was made to Nangi Maynard (as he was called by the Africans—Nangi means teacher) to go out to shoot a marauding lion or leopard. One day a call came to shoot a leopard which had been seen in a garden. Nangi Maynard picked up his gun and went.

In a letter written shortly afterwards, he described the encounter:

'Suddenly the leopard charged, roaring, and as she passed me, I fired at close range, knocking her completely over. She rose, whirling on me, and I fired again, missing. By that time she was on me, leaping for my face. I swept her to the ground by a blow from rifle and fist, but quick as a flash my left thigh was in her mouth, and my right leg in her left front paw. I seized her throat and literally tore her away from my leg, fortunately securing her right front paw with my other hand.

'We went down together, I on top, my right knee pinning her chest and right front leg. The Lord supplied sufficient strength for me to keep her absolutely helpless in that position, raging and gritting her teeth, until my cries induced a few men to come to my assistance. They seized her with a dozen hands, when I arose, and placing my rifle at her chest, shot her through the heart. I then gave the body (a large female) to men to bring home and then rode home on my bicycle, and truly I was glad when the journey ended.

'I have shot several leopards that had been driven up trees, but this is my first hand-to-tooth encounter, and the victory certainly was from God.'

So too was the provision to meet the need. Parcels took a very long time to reach their destination. Friends at home had despatched a parcel of surgical dressings shortly after the war ended. It had been delayed for many months, but finally reached the Doctor just at that time. They were used to treat her husband's wounds, which were very serious and for a long time would not heal. Wrote the doctor:

'If those dressings had reached here sooner, there would not have been a shred left to meet the present need.'

God's clocks are synchronized!

Although the number of missionary personnel was brought so low during the war years, the Lord of the harvest provided labourers in other ways. African workers were raised up in larger numbers than in any other field. They worked effectively, both in evangelism and teaching. Some went as far afield as 150 miles, preaching the Gospel in the villages. As converts were gathered, they instructed them and brought them to the central station for baptism.

Early in 1920 unusual blessing came to the Tanganyika field. The missionaries themselves were the first to be dealt with. They were humbled before the Lord, seeking His grace and deeper blessing. Many of the Christians also were deeply convicted of sin, and were impelled to make public confession of their failures. After a day or two, 'it seemed that the place, including all our hearts, had been swept by a healing, cleansing fire from the Lord', wrote Nangi, and the Lord's people were able to bear testimony to renewed joy in the Lord and power in service.

As an outcome of this, the message came with force to many. At that time three chiefs were among the large number who professed conversion.

One of these was an educated man and had been given the post of government school teacher by the Germans. But he was still a heathen, and when he became chief, he was a consistent and bitter persecutor of the four Christians among his people. During a time of famine, he commandeered the garden of one of these and thus deprived him of his only supply of food. At first the victim was justly indignant, but Nangi appealed to him to forgive the chief and to show love and to return good for evil.

It was not long before this bore fruit and the chief gave a hearing to the Christians, who preached Christ to him. They did this with increasing frequency and eventually the chief professed conversion.

Even though it was during the rains and he had to safari 24 miles through mud and water sometimes up to his armpits, he went to the mission station for the Sunday services and sought further instruction.

The pot containing the 'Medicine of the Chiefdom' was always kept in the chief's house. From its contents his witch-doctors concocted their charms against various illnesses. One night it disappeared. When the loss was discovered a great search was made, but it could not be found. This was a serious and alarming matter. The chief called all his councillors, witch-doctors and sub-chiefs to discover what had happened to the medicine.

A goat was solemnly sacrificed. Then they killed a chicken and consulted the entrails. From this they divined that a brother of the chief had stolen the medicine and was hatching a plot to discredit him before the Government and he himself be appointed chief in his place.

Thereupon the chief called for a hoe and led the procession to the place where he himself had buried the pot and unearthed it before them. He then told the people that he had done this to convince them that the diviners were liars and deceivers. He had given up these practices. He gave an order forbidding divining and rain-making in his territory. He killed the sacred bull, in which the spirits of his ancestors were said to dwell, and destroyed the rainhouse. This led to a big lawsuit, but many of the sub-chiefs decided to follow his lead. The chief, Wamba, was baptized in 1922.

Mr. Sywulka found himself in conflict with the witch-doctors more than once. In the course of one of his safaris he arrived at a chief's compound as an enquiry was being held to discover who had taken certain of the chief's possessions. After sacrifices had been made, the witch-doctor made all the people stand in line, holding their hands out before them. He then passed down the line muttering an incantation, holding a curved gourd over each hand in turn, explaining that when it came over the hand of the thief, water would spurt out of it. Mr. Sywulka watched the proceedings closely, especially as the 'thief' was shown to be an old man. At its close, he asked to see the instrument. He observed that a hole which was concealed by the thumb of the one who held the gourd controlled the flow of water. Without saying a word, Mr. Sywulka lined up the people again and went down the row just as the witch-doctor had done. But this time the people were astounded when water spurted over the hand of the chief's brother—thus indicating that he was the thief. Then the missionary let the people into the secret and showed them how the witch-doctor had deceived them. The crowd turned on the culprit and chased him from their midst.

The return of the Sywulkas in 1924 was timely. His spiritual outlook and godly example had much to do with the development of the church. He was constantly on safari among the Africans, travelling the countryside on his bicycle or on foot, with perhaps a critical eye on those who went in cars or lived in more comfortable houses. When he was with the Africans, he lived, slept and ate as they did.

He went from village to village telling the good news of salvation. Very many years after his homecall, one of the missionaries visited a village and told a heathen woman of the salvation which was available in Jesus Christ. The woman listened in silence. When the missionary stopped, she asked:

'Do you belong to Si Waka (the native name for Sywulka)? Many years ago he told me those words.'

She was still unconverted, but the words had remained in her memory through the years.

He was well known all over the countryside. In a remote

part, seldom visited by Europeans, a child began to scream with fright when he approached. The mother took the child up in her arms and said:

'Don't cry! That's not a Mazungu (European). That's Si Waka.'

Emil Sywulka loved his evangelists and held a week's Bible Course for them every three months—sometimes on a mission station, sometimes in one of the distant African churches. But he did not confine himself to Bible teaching. He taught them to sing in parts, using tonic-solfa; and to this day there are good choirs which sprang from his initiative. He wrote many hymns also. He would often sit up till midnight with his African friends around a log fire singing hymns.

He also prepared school material for them. In order to encourage afforestation he made each of his evangelists plant ten trees.

At testimony meetings which he promoted he invited the Christians to tell 'not what the Lord did for you years ago, but what He is doing for you now'.

A heart attack brought a sudden end to his activities on 7th November 1944. His passing was deeply lamented by African and European alike.

Only once did I meet Emil Sywulka personally. He was the main speaker at one of our conferences in Congo. The field was in an unhealthy condition. There were divisions, criticism and bitterness. Efforts to obtain a guest speaker had been unsuccessful. Some of us had been much in prayer for blessing.

Arriving at Aba in the late afternoon, we were introduced to a man who could never be called good-looking, dressed in black, with a huge Bible under his arm. It was Emil Sywulka. The Lord had provided a messenger for the occasion. He had hitch-hiked from Tanganyika and arrived on the field unheralded. He was asked to give daily talks at the coming conference. Visiting the stations in the interim, he heard all the criticisms, but said nothing.

At Aba, Emil Sywulka climbed to the top of the Aba Rock in the early mornings and spent hours in communion with the Lord. When he stood up to speak he brought with him, as he termed it, 'Grapes of Eshcol' he had gleaned in that quiet time. And what messages they were! He had his own original style. To this day I can never read the story of Abraham without thinking of him. He pictured what might have happened if Abraham and Sarah had been missionaries. He imagined a conversation between them criticizing Lot, bringing in all the bitter words he himself had heard as he visited the various stations. He built it up skilfully. Then he reminded his hearers that Abraham was not a missionary. Instead of being bitter, he went to Lot, probably putting his arms around him as he said:

'Let there be no strife, I pray thee, between me and thee . . . FOR WE BE BRETHREN' (Gen. 13 : 8).

Tenderly and courageously he pressed the lesson home. God used him to do a mighty work. Confessions of failure were made with tears and apologies tendered. A great change came over the whole field, and there has been a different spirit in it ever since.

Nangi Maynard was of a different type. Coming from a cultured family, he was quiet, gentle and refined, in contrast to the ruggedness of Emil Sywulka.

Yet his conversion, in adult life, had been dramatic. He described it in the following way:

'I had been a lover of good cigars and a frequenter of bars, a companion of others of like habits. True, I had been well taught from the Scriptures; but I was far from God.

'One night in Washington, D.C. (U.S.A.), I became so drunk that I couldn't remember anything. I was taken in by the police and charged with intoxication. A friend interceded for me and, with the help of the police, got me to my hotel room and to bed. The next morning my friend told me how near I had come to disgracing my family, respectable and honest people as they were.

'I still had a bottle of whiskey in my pocket, so I took a walk over near the Washington monument and threw the bottle as far as I could, smashing it to bits. I then and there decided that a change was necessary in my life. I could not continue with the gang of fellows with whom I had been associated. I must make a clean break.

'I got on a train going to St. Louis, and after two or three months there, connected myself with the Third Baptist Church where I served as an usher. I remember one Sunday morning coming down from the balcony, one of the deacons, a Mr. Guyett, threw his arms round me and said:

' "Jay, when are you going to take the Lord Jesus as your personal Saviour?"

' "Right now," I answered.

'We walked down the aisle together (as the custom is in many of our churches) and I received the Lord Jesus Christ as my Saviour. That evening I was baptized.

'There was an absolute and definite change in my life. The old things passed away right then and there, and another life took over. There was a gradual growth thereafter in my interest in the things of God until, fifteen years later, upon being married, my wife and I offered ourselves to God to become missionaries to Africa.'

Nangi Maynard did not go out to visit the Africans to the same extent that Mr. Sywulka did, except when he went to preach at the bush centres on Sundays; but his door was always open to receive them. They found it easy to pour their troubles into his sympathetic ears. He always sought to bring them to view their circumstances from a spiritual angle.

Many look to him as their spiritual father and friend. He did much to train the young men. Encouraged by him many African missionaries went to unreached parts to preach the Gospel. One went as far as Ukara, an island in Lake Victoria.

The Maynards had completed twelve years on the field before they went back to America on furlough. Their rest was taken on the voyages going and returning; for, while in the States, they were kept busy travelling from coast to coast telling of the work. A friend, Mrs. Young, in Wayne, Nebraska, arranged a drawing-room meeting at which the Doctor told the story of their twelve years in Africa, with its difficulties, trials, encouragements and hopes.

At the close of the meeting, the friend said to Dr. Maynard: 'Would you like to have a new hospital?'

Her mind went back to the little tent in which she had first worked, and then to the mud-and-wattle hut which had succeeded it, and to the miracles which God had wrought in them. Quietly she replied:

'If it is God's will. If He would continue the mighty miracles He has wrought in the little mud hut, then I would welcome a hospital with all my heart.'

At the close of a meeting at which Mrs. Young had ministered with signs of the Spirit's working, a young mother had been led into a life of victory. In her gratitude she had placed in Mrs. Young's lap a handful of beautiful diamonds to be used in making known the One Who had come to mean so much to her. After prayers, she felt that Dr. Maynard was the one to whom the gift should be given.

Provision was thus made for the hospital of her dreams. The furlough taken so reluctantly, and the busy months of deputation work, had been used of God to bring about His plans for the medical work at Kola Ndoto.

Another twenty years passed before the Maynards went on furlough again. They were called home to take part in the celebrations of the jubilee year of the Mission. The Second World War was being fought, and this brought many delays as they journeyed towards the States. After seven long months of travel they reached there, however, and could now tell of Jewel Hospital—the men's unit, a brick building, whitewashed, with metal roof, with its rows of beds, and a trained African staff of helpers. But beyond that was the Bethesda Hospital, the women's unit. Then the dispensary, with rooms for consultations, examinations, dispensing, etc. There was the leprosarium, housing over two hundred who were under treatment, many of whom had found deliverance from the sin of which leprosy is such a picture. Then there was the maternity hospital, where an average of 1,200 babies a year were born. To complete the picture were the Asiatic and European wards and the Children's Home. How much there was to tell! So much for which to praise the Lord! What great opportunities there were for further service! Younger workers were needed, and the Doctor sounded out the call.

She found the furlough tiring, however, and the voyage back brought no relief. Nine months after her return to the field in 1946 she became so weak that she had to give in and stay in bed. She was flown to Mwanza hospital where it was found that an operation would be necessary. But before it took place, the call came, and the little

Doctor went into the presence of the Lord she had served so devotedly.

So passed a valiant soul, though encased in a small body. Deeply spiritual, with a great love for the Africans, she was wise and foreseeing. As a matter of principle she would do nothing that an African could do.

'We are here,' said she, 'not so much to do the work, as to get it done.'

Another outstanding missionary in that field was Thomas G. Marsh. He became a well-known figure throughout the countryside as he travelled on his bicycle or motor-cycle. He visited existing churches and sought to get new ones started. He had a great burden for souls and was an inspiration to evangelists in areas distant from mission stations. He wrote:

'When I have been out in new areas, I have often got off my bicycle and claimed the place for the Lord as in Joshua 1 : 3. Then it was wonderful to see some young African volunteer to go out there to set up a little church.'

He was often asked to conduct Bible Conferences for Africans. The revision of the Sukuma New Testament claimed much of his attention. This translation had been commenced many years earlier, but never completed. The complete revision was finished in 1926.

Thomas Marsh longed for deeper blessing. Led by him, the missionaries pledged themselves to pray for revival. God has given times of blessing, but the full answer has not come yet.

The Africans knew him as a man of prayer. They remarked that the toes of his shoes turned up from much kneeling in prayer. Following his homecall in 1935, one of the African evangelists said: 'I want the knees of my trousers to wear out like those of Pastor Marsh.'

Mr. Maynard, writing of him, referred to 'The growing radiance of a life lived in Jesus Christ.'

His wife also was very active among women and girls. Their son and his wife are still at work on the field, carrying heavy responsibilities.

There were others too. William L. Downey went to Africa in 1921. During his twenty-two years of missionary service he opened the station at Buduhe. He typed the manuscript of the whole of the revised Kisukuma New Testament ready for printing. He also typed the first translation of a large part of the Old Testament.

While at Buduhe he pioneered into the little-known Bahi tribe. These people live in the depths of the forest and show many similarities to the pygmies in Congo. They have their own language, which incorporates many 'clicks', linking it with languages in South Africa. They were almost completely uninfluenced by the more progressive life of other tribes and were very suspicious of strangers.

A Bible-woman first drew his attention to them, and persuaded Mr. Downey to visit them. He found the chief very friendly and learned much of the customs and beliefs of the Bahi. Some of them knew Kisukuma, and he tried to teach them verses of Scripture; but it was the simple hymns which attracted them most.

Mr. Downey went to be with the Lord in 1943. No more safaris were made to the Bahi tribe for a long time. However, the Bible-woman met a relative of the chief. He told her that the chief had died. Said the man:

'His death was very strange, for, just before he died, he sang the song which the white man taught us:

' *"His grace is very great, His grace is very great.*
I praise Him, Jesus Christ." '

Mr. Downey was a very gracious and friendly man, beloved by all. After his homecall Mrs. Downey continued in the work until 1965. Their two daughters—one a nurse, the other a teacher—still serve the Lord in the country of their birth, Tanzania.

Mr. and Mrs. Whitlock were a couple whose work the Lord blessed. They went to Tanganyika in 1934 and took their first furlough in 1940. Many, both on the field and at home, looked to Paul Whitlock as one of the future leaders of the work. But God had other plans. On the completion of their furlough, they put their two eldest boys in school in America and left by air in January 1945 to return to Africa, taking the three younger sons with them. As the plane was about to land at Port of Spain, Trinidad, it suddenly plunged into the waters killing all on board. This was a severe shock, not only to Mrs. Whitlock's two sisters who were serving in Africa, and to the family at home, but to all. The whole Mission was stunned.

And what shall I say more? Limitations of time and space forbid me to tell of other worthy servants of the Lord—the Mannings, Mr. and Mrs. R. H. Baker, Mr. and Mrs. Hess, the Jesters, the Stiers, the Glocks and the noble army of single ladies who have done such faithful work in that field.

The work at Kola Ndoto hospital continues to grow. Dr. Arthur Barnett, Dr. Philip Morris, each served there for a time. Dr. Clifton Nelson and his wife, together with Dr. Martha Jeane Shaw, have been very fully occupied there in later years. Further buildings are still being added. A nurses' training school has been there for a number of years.

PART FOUR

CONGO

Pruned to Bear More

15

President, Professor and Poacher

MR. HURLBURT'S trip to America in 1908 had momentous consequences.

Following on the interview recorded above, President Theodore Roosevelt, released from office, fulfilled his long-cherished desire and went to Africa to shoot big game. During his time in East Africa he visited Kijabe and laid the corner-stone of the new school building of the Rift Valley Academy for the children of missionaries. He was deeply impressed with the work of the Mission.

For a long time the Bwana had had his eyes on that part of the Congo which lay in the line of advance envisaged by Peter C. Scott. But there had been grave difficulties in the way of entering there. It had seemed that the Enemy was determined that no invasion of this territory should be made by the forces of light. As ever, recourse was made to prayer. In answer, God moved President Roosevelt to use his influence with the Belgian Government and so permission to enter was obtained.

Anticipating in faith occupying this territory Bwana Hurlburt had been seeking information regarding it. The Lord had His man ready with it at the right time. As Messrs. Hurlburt and Stauffacher were on the Lake Victoria steamer at the end of the arduous safari into Tanganyika, they called at Bukoba, a port on the west side of the lake. There a stranger embarked. His appearance was rough, his beard ragged and it was obvious that he had spent a long time away from civilization. Yet in spite of his aspect, something proclaimed him the scholar. It was not long before they made his acquaintance and discovered that he was a Russian in the employ of a Berlin Anthropological Society. He had been studying the tribes in the Nile and Congo basins, and was returning after a sojourn of several months in the midst of the very people to whom they desired to go. Their enquiries interested him and immediately he threw open a vast fund of information of exactly the sort they wanted. They spent the whole afternoon and evening copying maps and writing down material. Their hearts were filled with praises as they saw in this the answer to the prayers of many years.

Not until the Stauffachers returned after their first furlough could a trip to Congo be made. Bwana Hurlburt himself had hoped to go with John, but urgent business necessitated a visit to America. He arranged for Mr. Gribble to take his place.

Accordingly a start was made in May 1910. They travelled by way of Kampala in Uganda, with five porters who promised to accompany them for the whole of the safari. With such a small retinue they could only take the barest minimum. Having a tent and blankets to be carried, they took nothing more than a few beads for presents and some tins of provisions.

A call was made on Bishop Tucker. They hoped to get some encouragement and helpful advice from one who was so experienced; but when they told him of their plans he gave little comfort. After putting them up for the night, he said:

'I don't want to discourage you, but don't you realize that our Society (the Church Missionary Society was a strong and influential Society in Uganda) has been trying for a long time to get into Congo and that we have sent parties there with as many as two hundred porters and military escorts? Yet we have not succeeded in establishing ourselves there. How then can you hope to do anything with this small band?'

The two pioneers realized the force of his arguments, but stammering out a few apologetic words, they said they felt they must go on and try.

After the first day's safari they began to feel that they were on a foolish errand. There were no roads and they lost the path. And to make matters worse, Mr. Gribble developed an attack of malaria with a high temperature.

The attack of malaria was soon over and the next day they set out again. But that was not the end of their discouragements. When they reached the C.M.S. station of Hoima, after ten days of hard safari across Uganda, they learned that the British, who had just taken over the West Nile District from the Belgians, had placed the whole area under quarantine for sleeping sickness, and all access was forbidden. That seemed to be their last hope dashed to the ground.

The Rev.* and Mrs. Lloyd, who were in charge of the station, invited them to stay with them for a few days. There they were, within 30 miles of Lake Albert, but the way seemed blocked.

Several days later Mr. Lloyd was giving a graphic description of a fishing trip he had taken towards the southern end of Lake Albert, when suddenly he stopped and said:

'How silly of me not to think of it before. If you want to go to Belgian Congo, why don't you go south instead of north? There is nothing to hinder you going in there, except . . .' and he did not finish the sentence.

---

* Archdeacon Lloyd (as he later became) was the uncle of Rev. T. E. Lloyd, who is Home Secretary of the British Home Council.

They were off the next morning. Three days safari brought them to a very high escarpment overlooking the lake. They sat on a rock and feasted their eyes on a view which few Europeans had gazed on up to that time. Almost the whole of Lake Albert lay before them. To the south was the Semliki River winding back and forth until it was lost to view among the foothills of Mount Ruwenzori, the famous Mountains of the Moon. Opposite them on the other side of the lake were the hills which constituted their first sight of Congo—hills on which several of our mission stations now stand.

It was thrilling. They did not spend much time admiring the scene, however, but hurried down the rocky escarpment to the plains below. Antelope abounded in great variety. The travellers camped on the shores of the lake, but their sleep was disturbed by the splashing and grunting of hippopotami feeding on the shore.

The next morning they pushed on in a southerly direction and reached the banks of the Semliki River. On the other side was Belgian Congo.

But they sensed trouble among their porters, who up to that time had been surprisingly good-tempered. They were sullen. A storm which broke that afternoon did not help matters. The whole sky darkened, and there was an ominous stillness. Then a strong wind sprang up which brought the rain, with crashing thunder, and vivid lightning. The two men sheltered in their tent as the storm spent itself. Suddenly the tent was ripped open from end to end, and they were left exposed to the teeming rain. The porters came from a native hut some distance away and helped them in their predicament.

When the storm was over, the porters said that the natives had told them that if they attempted to cross the Semliki they would all be killed.

'That probably would have happened had we all tried to cross over,' wrote Mr. Stauffacher, 'and certainly would have happened had we tried to cross with two hundred porters and some native soldiers.'

The two missionaries decided, however, to press on, but they packed up their goods and told the porters to take them back to Hoima and wait there.

They found a man with a canoe who, in return for a few beads, took them across the river.

A crowd of natives on the opposite bank stood ready to oppose their coming; but when they saw only a couple of unarmed men they allowed them to land. So the Africa Inland Mission made its first appearance in Congo. They landed with much trepidation, not knowing what awaited them. Their apprehension seemed to be confirmed, for the people in the nearby village looked extremely unpleasant. But just when they thought that their fears of the worst were about to be realized, who should appear but two Africans dressed in a sort of uniform, with guns on their shoulders. The soldiers asked the newcomers who they were. 'Missionaries,' they replied. The soldiers laughed and turning to the crowd around them pointed out that the two men had nothing but sticks in their hands. Then to the utter astonishment of the missionaries they informed them that their 'Bwana' was waiting for them on the path going up the escarpment. Led by the soldiers the two men made their way along the steep and tortuous path wondering who the 'Bwana' could possibly be. At length they came to a figure sitting on a rock. He was red-headed, and had red whiskers all over his face. As soon as he began to speak they knew he was Irish. When he saw them he laughed long and loud.

'I know who you are,' he said, 'you're missionaries

and probably the only people in Africa who could come
in here now. I saw you down by the river. I thought
you might be policemen coming here for such as me.
If you had been, I should certainly have tried to stop
you. Or, thought I, you might be hunters and might
have a bit of ammunition to spare, for even my soldiers
are carrying empty guns.'

He was one of a band of the most unusual adventurers
one could ever wish to meet. These men were living in
this disputed territory and hunting elephant. They had
set up their own government and collected taxes in the
form of ivory. They were monarchs of all they surveyed.

The burly Irishman climbed down from his rock and
led them to his camp. They discovered that he had a small
herd of cattle, a plentiful supply of food and an African
wife whom he called Annie. She spoke English well and
ran the house very efficiently. He invited them to stay
with him as long as they wished. But later he informed
them that the Belgian authorities were after him, and
in a few days he would have to leave there for good. He
offered to let them have all his possessions if they wished
to remain. His camp was within a few miles of the site
where later on the Bogoro mission station was established.

As they sat round the dinner table that evening, he told
them his plans. He would go northward along the shores
of the lake in dugout canoes which he owned, and then
make his way into Uganda, and try to escape the police of
both British and Belgians. He said they were welcome to
accompany him if they were prepared to run the risk of
being arrested as elephant poachers. He was very nervous
and expected to be caught any moment. It turned out,
however, that they were doing him a favour for they had
in their possession a letter from King Albert of Belgium
asking all government servants to assist them wherever

possible. They decided to go with him.

Down to the lake they went, and were surprised to find half a dozen dugout canoes placed at their disposal. There was abundance of food for the trip and they feasted on fish, bananas, sweet potatoes and occasionally eggs and chickens. Annie was an excellent cook and provided them with all kinds of tasty dishes. What surprised them most, however, was that she kept them supplied with good white bread, although they had no idea where the flour came from.

'Imagine our feelings,' recorded John, 'as we were travelling in perfect comfort with a man who knew the country perfectly and who could give us information concerning both the natives and the land beyond us which could not then have been obtained in any other way. Surely an all-seeing eye was conscious of all our needs and we could not but rejoice in thinking of it in that way. I don't think I shall ever forget that journey, for the western shores of Lake Albert are very beautiful. A very high escarpment runs for the whole distance until it nearly reaches the banks of the Nile River. Beautiful forest trees abound down to the very rocks on the lake shore. Now and then rivers and small streams come tumbling down forming beautiful waterfalls. Hippos could be seen almost continually and often we could see on ahead what looked like rocks above the surface of the water, but when we would get close up the rocks would begin to tumble and disappear beneath the surface. The fish were most interesting and we saw some that probably weighed about a hundred pounds. Native fishermen were found everywhere and they never hesitated to give us all we needed.'

After travelling in this fashion for several days, they

caught sight of the buildings of Mahagi Port. They felt that they should go to pay their respects to the Belgian officials there. Their host did his best to dissuade them, saying that if they went they would not be allowed to return for they were in forbidden territory. But when he saw that their minds were set, he agreed to let them go, asking them to return as soon as possible, for he was afraid to wait long. They were received very graciously by the officials. When they returned to the lakeside, however, they were dismayed to find no sign whatever of their host or the fleet of canoes. They had disappeared completely!

After a little while, one of the rowers appeared furtively out of the grass. He informed them that one of the canoes was hidden among the papyrus, but all the others had struck across the lake towards Uganda. They entered the canoe and followed. Before night they found their Irish host encamped on a small island on the Uganda side.

The next day they went down the Nile, which runs out of Lake Albert, and reached a place which was occupied by a few Britishers. Here the poacher found that he would be safe on the British side, so he decided to remain there. A small tug, which had brought supplies, was returning to Butiaba on the Uganda side the next day. The two missionaries embarked on it.

Looking back later they wondered why they had not made their way farther into Congo to reach the Azande tribe, for that had been their objective when they set out. They were, however, without supplies or other resources. Moreover, they were so full of enthusiasm over the possibilities they had discovered for missionary endeavour, that all they wanted to do was to go back and report. Today, almost within sight of the course they followed, there are ten mission stations.

Reaching Butiaba about noon, they left the tug and walked along the shore. The heat seemed overpowering.

They found an unoccupied hut and went into it to discuss their plans. They had a season of prayer for guidance. As Mr. Gribble was praying at some length, they heard sudden shouts of 'Jambo, Jambo' (the Swahili greeting). They came from the five porters they had left several weeks earlier on the banks of the Semliki. It was a happy reunion. Before long they were on their way with their own beds and blankets again. They felt as rich as kings.

The following day they were back at Hoima telling the Lloyds the story of their adventures. A further ten days on foot brought them to Kampala again. Their funds were exhausted, and John was ill with malaria, and they were cast upon the Lord. But when they called on the Bishop they discovered to their relief that he had a letter for them which contained enough money to see them back to Kijabe. They arrived there exactly three months and one day after they had set out.

16

Entrance

IT was not until 1912 that any further attempt to enter Congo was possible. The party consisted of Bwana Hurlburt, Dr. Newberry, the Stauffachers and their two sons, Mr. Patton, who was acting as private secretary to Mr. Hurlburt, Mr. and Mrs. Haas and baby and Miss Harland.

The S.S. *Samuel Baker* was making her first trip on Lake Albert and they were able to take advantage of it. The crossing took only a few hours and the party arrived at Mahagi Port, Congo, on 20th April 1912, and prepared to pitch their camp on the very spot where the two pioneers had landed nearly eighteen months earlier.

They were quite ignorant of the fact that Mahagi Port was still closed to outsiders. The captain of the *Samuel Baker* had known it, however, but had not told them. Instead he perpetrated an amusing trick. Unknown to the missionaries, he sent a message to the Belgian Chef de Poste informing him that the Governor of Uganda had arrived! The ship then left without waiting for any further developments. It was not long before a rather confused official arrived, dressed in his best white uniform and carrying a glittering sword, making the most profuse bows to Mr. Hurlburt who seemed to be the head of the party and therefore the Governor of Uganda! But seeing the women and children he realized that there had been a mistake. When he discovered that it was a party of missionaries, he laughed heartily and told them what the captain had done. The captain's ruse saved them a lot of trouble, for had the official witnessed the arrival of the boat, he would have had to refuse the group permission to land. As it was, he invited them all to dinner that evening. Knowing little of the principles held by the missionaries he was highly amused to discover that they would take no alcoholic drinks! The official did all he could to help them, as did others, and when, later, he moved away from Mahagi, they felt they were losing a very good friend.

The first plan was that the whole party should proceed to the Azande tribe, and there open the first Congo station. Then the Stauffachers could return to Mahagi and open a station in that area to provide a link in the route to the interior. But they found that the porters and canoemen were demanding much higher wages than they were prepared to pay.

They decided to look for a site for a mission station near Mahagi and postpone all thought of proceeding to Azande country. By this time the Bwana felt he should return to Kenya and go on to America and England on Mission business. So he borrowed a sailing boat belonging to the Belgian official who had been so kind to them and went back across the lake.

The same official placed a three-roomed grass hut at the disposal of the party. They managed to squeeze into the cramped accommodation it offered. Their immediate troubles appeared to be over. But on the second night of their residence there, a torrential storm arose and the whole house collapsed over their heads.

Other difficulties arose, however. Stealing became a major problem. In spite of all the precautions they adopted, their goods disappeared at an alarming rate. One lady awoke one morning to find that everything of hers had been taken and apart from her night-clothes and the blankets on her bed she was left with nothing. During it all she had slept soundly! The thieves became so bold that they would almost snatch things from the hands of the missionaries. When the matter was reported to the official, he said that they should shoot to kill; nothing else would frighten the thieves. But they could not consider such a thing. One member of the party decided to nail up his place with bamboo, and to stack all his boxes at the head of his bed. But the thieves managed to cut a hole in the bamboo while he was asleep. A few days before it was required they stole his wedding outfit!

In the meantime reinforcements had arrived from Great Britain. The fact that Peter Cameron Scott had been born in Scotland, had re-dedicated himself to Africa in Westminster Abbey, had known personally Hudson Taylor, founder of the China Inland Mission, already provided a link between the Council in America and British friends. This was strengthened when Mr. Hurlburt visited England in 1904. He had the opportunity of giving a short missionary address at the Keswick Convention. As a result, a small committee was set up under the chairmanship of the Rev. J. Stuart Holden. Mr. Hurlburt again visited England in 1911, and at that time the committee was increased by the addition of a number of well-known Christian leaders.

Through Mr. Hurlburt's ministry at Keswick and at Cambridge University, a number of undergraduates were called to the mission field. Among these was Rev. G. F. B. Morris, who was curate to Rev. J. Stuart Holden, at St. Paul's, Portman Square, London. For a short time, Mr. Morris acted as Honorary Home Secretary to the Mission.

Fred Morris had studied at Ridley Hall, after graduating from Queens' College, Cambridge. He was elected President of the Cambridge Inter-collegiate Christian Union while there. His ordination took place in 1910.

Another was Rev. J. Batstone, a fellow-undergraduate of Mr. Morris. A third was C. T. Studd, the well-known England cricketer, who had already seen service in China with the China Inland Mission. These with others formed a party which set out from England early in 1913. Before they reached Kijabe, however, Mr. Studd decided to found his own mission in Congo.

In view of this situation, the following letter was sent out by the British Home Council:

Dear Friends,

At a meeting of the A.I.M. Council held on 3rd March, some members who are special friends of Mr. C. T. Studd stated that they had learned from him that he felt unable to continue his relationship with the A.I.M. unless radical changes were made in the constitution.

After careful consideration it was found that it would be impossible to make such changes, and indeed those who had been for some time connected with the work deemed them undesirable and unnecessary. These friends, therefore, presented Mr. Studd's resignation from the A.I.M. and have formed themselves into a new body to represent him, as he continues to work in the Belgian Congo on independent lines. We have learned by cable that of the party which went out last month Messrs. G. F. B. Morris, J. Batstone and W. Rampley have decided to remain with the A.I.M.; Mr. A. B. Buxton continuing with Mr. Studd . . .

We invite the earnest prayers of all friends of the mission for our brethren who have formed the new Mission and for our brothers Messrs. G. F. B. Morris, J. Batstone and W. Rampley, who represent us on the field. Let us ask that God will send forth many trained workers to join them, and raise up many at home whose

sympathy and prayers will sustain them in their difficult work.

> J. Stuart Holden (President)
> D. P. Robinson (Hon. Home Director)
> C. E. Hurlburt (General Director)

17th March 1913.

Mr. Studd proceeded to Congo with Alfred Buxton, who
was engaged to Mr. Studd's daughter. When they reached
Congo, however, they were informed that while permission had been given for the A.I.M. to start work there,
no such entry could be granted to another Mission. It was
therefore agreed that they should enter under the aegis of
the A.I.M. and if, later, they wanted to form a separate
body, they would be at liberty to do so. They stayed at
Mahagi while awaiting the large party of porters required
to carry their goods. Mr. Gribble accompanied them on
the first part of their safari in order to help them.

In May 1913 another British party sailed and arrived
at Kasengu on 22nd July. These included D. M. Miller
(later for many years Secretary in England), Mr. J. Clarke,
Madge Hurst, who was engaged to Fred Morris, and Sarah
Stirton. Mr. Hurlburt had expected to travel to Congo
with these reinforcements, but illness prevented him. So
John Stauffacher accompanied them up-country to help
find a suitable site for a station. They found it impossible
to obtain sufficient porters to carry their goods, and much
equipment had to be left behind. Moreover, the porters
were unreliable, and were not willing to enter the territory of another tribe. Often, indeed, after they had
travelled but a few miles they would put their loads down,
demand their pay and go home. Because of this, the group
found themselves only two or three days away from
Kasengu after two weeks of travel. However, facing the
hazards of flooded rivers, wild animals, in addition to the

untrustworthiness of the porters and their own uncertain health, they plodded on. As they travelled onwards, they found that help was more easily obtainable. Government resthouses, simply built and of temporary materials, were situated at regular intervals. These provided them with shelter and made their way easier.

They were surprised to find little shops here and there, owned by Greek or Indian traders, and there they could often buy supplies of tinned foods.

They eventually reached Faradje on the fringe of the Azande tribe about 16th September.

They tramped another 90 miles and, on 24th September, reached Dungu. They were astounded to find a thriving government post there, with several Greek and Belgian shops catering not only for local Africans but for travellers and government officials. While they were seeking for a site one of the Greek merchants gave them the use of a brick house. They felt that this was a great luxury.

Fred Morris went to pay his respects to the Chef de Zone, the highest of the officials there. He was a Count, and was very friendly to the missionaries. He invited the party to his house for five o'clock tea and made them a present of a fish weighing fifty pounds which had been caught in the nearby Dungu River.

About 2 miles from the post they discovered a suitable location. It was on one of the very few hills in the district and had a river running below it. Wrote John Stauffacher at that time:

'Up to the time we opened our station at Dungu there was not one Protestant mission station all the way from Lake Albert to Lake Chad, a country occupied by millions of natives.'

The next day C. T. Studd and Alfred Buxton arrived. They stayed that night, but seeing that the A.I.M. was already planning to establish work at Dungu they pressed on to Niangara and beyond to open up work for the Mission they were inaugurating.

The Stauffachers, anxious for the welfare of their two children whom they had left at Kasengu, started out again after a few days. They had to face similar difficulties as on the way up, but at length a little short of two months after they had left, they arrived back.

Between intermittent attacks of malaria, the British party set to work to erect houses and other buildings on the Dungu site.

It was not long before Bwana Hurlburt, whose heart was ever in the front line of advance, went to Congo to inspect the new work. He was greatly impressed by what had been done, but longed to press on still farther to reach the unevangelized peoples.

By the end of 1915 work had also been opened at Bafuka (later called Napopo), and Yakaluku. Progress had been made in the study of the Azande language.

The very mention of Congo conjures in the minds of many a picture of hot steamy swamps, with coconut palms and rubber plantations. True as this may be of certain parts of that huge territory, it is by no means correct of the north-eastern section where the A.I.M. works. But, then, it must be borne in mind that the Republic of Congo covers over 900,000 square miles of territory; that its north-eastern boundary is almost 1,500 miles from the west coast and 1,200 miles from Katanga, which in its turn is roughly the same distance from the coast. That is to say that if London were where the mouth of the Congo River vomits its filthy waters into the Atlantic, the A.I.M. station of Aba would be somewhere near Moscow and the southern boundary close to Athens. A large part of Congo's eastern boundary is the watershed of Central Africa. It is this range which forms the western escarpment of Lake

Albert and the other lakes farther south.

A number of A.I.M. stations are built on this ridge. The altitude rises to 7,000 feet and more, and those stations can be very cold, although very beautiful. The soil is rich and fertile. Other stations are lower and correspondingly hotter, until they reach the lowest in Azande country; but even there the altitude is over 1,000 feet.

The scenery varies also. Entering the A.I.M. area from the south one finds the pygmy forest with tall trees and almost impenetrable undergrowth. Mount Ruwenzori, just over the Uganda border, looks down on almost unbroken forest stretching westwards for hundreds of miles. But northwards the scene gradually opens out into farming country with patches of forest here and there. Farther north still is the savannah country, with fewer trees and leading on to the hotter and more tropical appearance of Azande land.

Until about 1930 there were hardly any motor roads, and all travel was on bush paths trodden out by the feet of men. But after that time, the country was opened up with a number of main routes. These were kept in reasonably good order until the last few years, when disturbed conditions and financial shortage have resulted in their being neglected, and now they are in a deplorable state. Missionaries use them, however. They have to, for there is no other way of transporting their supplies; but the toll on their vehicles is very heavy. There is now an M.A.F. plane stationed at Bunia, and whenever possible this is used; but it cannot carry much. One of the conditions for reoccupation of the Congo stations was that there should be an airstrip near each missionary post. There also had to be a radio link-up throughout the field.

17

Advance

THE work in Congo leapt ahead. The missionary staff was augmented and new stations opened even during the war years. In 1918 work was started at Aba, near the Sudan border.

In view of this advance, Mr. Hurlburt felt that Kijabe was too far east to be suitable as the headquarters of the Mission. Accordingly the office of the Central Executive Council was transferred to Aba in 1919. The Kenya and Tanganyika fields were placed under Field Directors. These were to pay periodic visits to Aba to transact business common to all three fields. As the fields were so far apart, however, and transport in those days was poor, this was found to be impracticable, and the three areas became separate and independent.

Aba is a delightful station, situated on a rise which dominates all the surrounding country. On the top of the hill is a huge rock. Mr. Hurlburt and many since have climbed there to find quiet for prayer. The red ironstone of the soil, the fresh green of Aba's vegetation during the greater part of the year and the richer green of the mango trees which line its paths make an impressive picture. This attractive site remained the headquarters of the Congo field for many years. Later, however, this was transferred to Rethy, a station which is much higher, healthier and cooler.

Reference has already been made to Mr. D. M. Miller. D. M. Miller was a Scot, born at Rothesay in 1888. After leaving school he trained as a cabinet-maker, although he never followed this for a livelihood. Converted at the age of sixteen, he soon heard the call of God to whole-time service. In due time he took training with the Faith Mission, and afterwards served as an evangelist both in Scotland and Northern Ireland. When Mr. Hurlburt visited Britain D. M. Miller heard the Spirit's call and applied to the Africa Inland Mission.

He sailed in 1913 to Mombasa and proceeded inland by train. When they reached Kikuyu, Mr. Hurlburt pulled him off to attend the Kikuyu Conference on Missionary Co-operation. There he heard an address by Bishop Peel of Mombasa which set the course for the whole of his life. Speaking on Job 26: 14 (R.V.), 'How small a whisper is heard of Him', he said:

'What is heard in your life? Is it the sound of the hammer, or the bustle of self-importance and feverish activity? Or is it the voice of God? We are here to make God heard.'

D. M. Miller, for his part, resolved that from thenceforth the aim of his life would be that, from the quiet of a God-possessed life, he might make God heard.

He became one of the pioneer missionaries in Congo, and played a large part in the opening of the work in the Azande tribe. In 1916 he went to the Logo tribe and opened Moldisa, a station south of Aba. The Logo work was later centred at Todro.

D. M. Miller was a careful workman and builder. Although the houses he erected were often of poles and mud, they were precisely and beautifully finished. Some of the furniture he made was in constant use by other missionaries—including myself—until recently.

In 1917, 'D.M.M.', as he was later called, married Miss Catherine Mozley, one of three sisters who served with the A.I.M. in Congo. The Millers had to leave the field in 1923, shortly after returning from their first furlough, on account of Mrs. Miller's health. After a period as Deputation Secretary, Mr. Miller became Secretary in Great Britain. He held this post until his retirement in 1956. His quiet dignity and graciousness, combined with deep spirituality, made their impact on the evangelical community, and the A.I.M. became better known. It was often referred to as 'D. M. Miller's Mission'.

Retirement did not mean any lessening of interest in Africa. He remained an active member of Council until his homecall in 1965. He was burdened with the need of literature for Africans and did all he could to encourage its production and distribution. He had many other interests in the Lord's work.

In the early 1920s, the Congo field, and Mr. Hurlburt personally, suffered severe bereavements. During that time a group of three friends passed away. The first of the group was Alta Hurlburt. She was her father's right hand, and seemed indispensable. While passing through London in 1921 in company with her father, she fell a prey to blackwater fever, the disease which carried off so many missionaries in the early days of the work. Two years later, Dr. Elizabeth Morse Hurlburt, her very close friend who had married Paul, the Bwana's son, passed away at Aba from the same disease. She left two young children. Mary Mozley looked after these, but ten months later she, too, succumbed. These three were esteemed not alone for the work they did but for their own lives. Each was a devoted servant of the Lord and refined in character. They were those who, humanly speaking, could least be spared.

A name which has appeared on the roll of Congo missionaries longer than any other is that of Floyd Pierson. Richard Floyd Pierson came to the field at an earlier age than any other, in 1917. He already had two sisters on the field. After serving for a while in Kenya, and helping in the early work of the West Nile District, Uganda, he went to Congo. He and his sister Flora (afterwards Mrs. Kemptner) worked at Bafuka in the Azande tribe. In 1927 when Paul Hurlburt left the field, Floyd took his place as Field Director of the Congo. There were few motor roads then, but he travelled faithfully from one end to the other of the Congo field of those days, on bicycle or on foot, and latterly by motor-cycle. Every station was visited in the course of his itineraries. By whatever means he travelled he always contrived to reach the mission station clean as a new pin. How he managed it we never discovered. We could only surmise that he stopped at a convenient place before reaching the station and spruced up.

It came as a surprise to nearly all the missionaries when, in 1926, he announced his engagement to Amy Winsor. The secret had been well kept. She was a teacher from Wheaton College, Illinois, and the first of three sisters and a brother who served with the A.I.M. in Congo. They were married later in the year.

In 1925 Mr. Hurlburt realized that his failing health would no longer permit him to carry the heavy responsibilities of General Director with the expanding work in the homelands and on the field. He therefore resigned, but accepted the position of General Director Emeritus. It was officially explained that:

'Mr. Hurlburt's resignation from the post of General Director does not in any way indicate a severance of his hopes, affections, and such strength as he has from the Mission and its interests which have been the very life-centre of his prayers, thoughts and energies for so many years. He expects to be able to serve the cause in a capacity less prominent, though equally necessary, and has offered to hold himself entirely at the disposal of his successor for help, information and advice, as long as such is needed.'

The Home Council for North America passed the following resolution:

'Whereas, In the providence of God Charles E. Hurlburt, the General Director of the Africa Inland Mission, has felt compelled to resign from this position because of physical infirmities, and persists in the conviction that this is God's will for him, we, the Home Council of the Africa Inland Mission, having after earnest prayer accepted his resignation, now wish to record:

'*First:* Our sincere thanks to almighty God for His rich gift to the Mission in the life and service of this consecrated servant.

'*Second:* Our appreciation of the wonderful vision and passion for the evangelization of Africa given him, and especially for the loyalty, devotion and self-sacrifice with which he has literally devoted his life to the carrying out of this vision almost from the very inception of the Mission.

'*Third:* We would further gratefully recognize the real greatness of this servant of God and of the service which he rendered to the whole cause of Christ in Africa. We adopt as our own the estimate given of him by the late Theodore Roosevelt when he said he was the greatest man he had met in Africa, and the conviction expressed by Dr. Stuart Holden when he declared that when Hurlburt is given his final place in history he will rank with the immortals of the missionary world.

'*Fourth:* We hereby express our sincere desire for continued fellowship with him in prayer and the hope that the great wealth of his knowledge of the Field and the Mission and his wise counsel may continue at the disposal of the Council and the Mission to the extent that his health may permit. We also most earnestly covet the privilege of fellowship with him in caring for his material needs to the end of the day.

'*Finally:* We unite in assuring our dear brother and fellow-worker of our love, tender affection and heartfelt sympathy in his sickness and that daily our prayers shall ascend in his behalf. In this we affectionately commend him to the love and comfort of Him who is touched with the feeling of our infirmities. It is hereby

'*Resolved:* That these resolutions be spread on our minutes and that a copy thereof be forwarded to Mr. Hurlburt.'

For a time after his resignation, Mr. Hurlburt was pastor of a small Baptist church in Garden Grove, California. Later he accepted the post of Superintendent of the Bible Institute of Los Angeles, holding it for about two years. After that he preached in various churches as he was invited.

In later years Mr. Hurlburt suffered from very severe headaches. Operations relieved them for a time.

He passed away in 1936 and was laid to rest in Forest Lawn Cemetery, Glendale, California.

Mr. Hurlburt was also instrumental in the formation of the Unevangelized Africa Mission which opened work in Congo, and later merged with the Conservative Baptist Missionary Society.

Mrs. Hurlburt outlived her husband and spent the declining years of her life with her daughter Mrs. Agnes Bell at the A.I.M. station of Oicha, radiating sweetness to all who knew her. Her body rests among the forest trees there.

In 1928 Floyd introduced Mr. Van Dusen into the work of Field Director, and the following spring, the Piersons went on furlough. They returned to Aba and Floyd was Station Superintendent for some years until they were asked to open a new station among the Azande tribe. It was the most westerly station of the Congo field, at Assa. This involved much arduous work. The people were unstable and unresponsive. There was much disease, and it seemed as if this had dulled their mentality. Floyd Pierson is a great hunter, expert in tracking game and a first-rate shot. This pleased the Azande and gained their confidence. They were always ready to accompany him on his hunts and to lead him to the herds of elephant and buffalo in those parts.

Although not a gifted preacher, he uses every occasion to bring the Gospel before the people. Amy Pierson started a school. Simple medical work opened up great possibilities, and in course of time a nurse was appointed to work with them. Every now and again a doctor visits the station. In anticipation of this, hundreds of patients needing surgery come and wait. They are thus brought under the sound of the Gospel and many hear it for the first time.

Work was also commenced among the many suffering from leprosy as on a number of other stations and in course of time a large colony was established, with its own dispensary and church buildings. The sight of these people calls forth sympathy and joy. Sympathy at the sight of their deformities; joy, that they can be under such care and treatment and hear the message of God's love.

Mr. Van Dusen remained in office for thirty years, apart from furloughs. George and Margaret Van Dusen were converted in adult life, after their marriage. He had been a successful businessman, and had passed advanced examinations in finance. Hearing the call of the Lord to service in Africa, they sold their home and business in order to pay for their training and other expenses in going forth.

After serving some years at Todro among the Logo tribe, he was appointed Field Director in 1928. It was a position for which he was well fitted. He led, not by the exercise of authority but by virtue of a humble walk with God and the influence of his character. He held this position until within one month of his death. Mr. Van Dusen served everybody. He visited every station in the Congo field—on foot where necessary. I remember walking about 50 miles with him to visit the station which had just opened among the foothills of Mount Ruwenzori. But travel by bicycle, motor-cycle and later by car was undertaken by him in order that he might help all stations. It was not generally known that for the greater part of his time he would not draw on Mission funds to pay for his journeys, but looked to the Lord to supply in other ways. Frequently he transported needed supplies or goods belonging to the missionaries and they were only too glad to repay the cost, which was considerably less than hired transport, even if that were available. As he visited station after station the burdens of the work and of the missionaries' private experiences were confided to him. He was always ready to give sound and spiritual advice.

His business knowledge was used to the great advantage of the Mission. Almost to the last he carried the burden of the work of Field Treasurer—no mean task when added to that of Field Director and sometimes that of Station Superintendent as well.

'Bwana Van', as we called him affectionately, was the friend of missionaries and Africans alike—a most lovable man. After a long period of suffering his wife Margaret passed away at Oicha Hospital in 1940. She was interred in the cemetery there amid the giant forest trees. Later he married Doris Groat, a Canadian schoolteacher and girls' worker. There were no children from his first marriage. He had two daughters by his second wife.

The secret of Bwana Van's usefulness lay in his morning tryst with the Lord. His day commenced with a time of reading of the Word and communion with his God. He did not regard himself as a preacher. When therefore he was called upon to speak, he was very much cast upon the Lord. In consequence, his messages found a more permanent place in our memories than those of some more gifted ministers. They seemed to stick.

Bwana Van was a man of iron constitution. Apart from infrequent bouts of malaria—which everyone suffers from in Congo—he was rarely ill. This may have tempted him to overtax his strength latterly, forgetting that he was approaching seventy years of age.

He rarely missed the prayer meeting on Rethy station. It was as he was walking home from it one day in July 1958 that he was taken ill. Only with the greatest difficulty could he drag himself over the remaining distance to his house. He took to his bed. A few days later I went to Rethy to visit him.

'My work is finished,' said he. He did not appear to be as seriously ill as his words suggested, and I did my best to cheer him up. I had prayer with him, which he appreciated. But his condition did not satisfy the doctors. Eventually Dr. Becker took him to Oicha where he could have him under his immediate care.

It was in October 1958 that the word went out over the radio network of the Mission that Bwana Van was 'absent from the body; present with the Lord'. A wave of sorrow passed over the whole field. As many as were within reach made their way to Oicha for the funeral. It was more than a coincidence that four Congolese pastors, representing various areas of the Congo church, were present, and carried the body to its resting place beside his first wife. How Bwana Van would have rejoiced to know that Yoane Akudri, an outstanding African pastor, whom he had baptized thirty years before, brought a message at the graveside.

Great changes had taken place during Mr. Van Dusen's years on the field. He had led the work through a critical period. The small beginnings had grown into a rich harvest, with the Lord's blessing.

18

Uncle John

WE must now retrace our steps to consider one who was a true pioneer missionary and who played a large part in the early days in Congo, in the West Nile District of Uganda, in opening up the work in what is now the Central African Republic, and in the Sudan—John G. Buyse.

'Uncle John' had been born in Holland in 1883. The home was a humble one, but it was one in which God was honoured. The parents had a large family and it was their constant prayer that their children might be brought to the knowledge of the Lord.

Leaving school at an early age, John was apprenticed to a house painter; but he longed to go to sea and become a pilot. When he was fifteen, his father gave him permission to go; but he did so reluctantly, for John did not yet know Christ as his Saviour. Life on the old windjammers was hard, and temptations abounded, and his parents followed him with earnest and anxious prayers. From time to time he came home, and told tales of life at sea and of the countries he had visited. But he did not stay long. The salt sea air was in his blood and he was off again. And still the parents prayed on.

He did not write often, but when he did, his letters were hailed with joy. The crowning occasion came when he wrote from Canada as his ship was unloading her cargo, telling how, in mid-ocean, he had come to Christ. The parents' faith had been rewarded.

He was eager for fellowship, and wherever his ship called, he sought out the Seamen's Mission.

One day, as he was at the helm of his ship, the Lord spoke to John about giving his whole life to His service. His response was immediate. He left the sea, dedicated to the work of the Lord. When he told his parents, they disclosed that they had given him to the Lord before his birth. He went to America for Bible training.

There he heard the Lord's call to Africa, and applied to the Africa Inland Mission. Before leaving for the field in 1916, he married.

The couple went to Congo and were assigned to work at Ara, a station high up in the hills overlooking Lake Albert, among the Alur tribe. John Buyse was greatly used there and, with another missionary, was instrumental in leading two Belgian officials to the Lord.

But the end of his first year on the field found John stricken in heart. His young wife had died in childbirth. She was buried with the babe in her arms. He wrote:

'The Lord has taken all that was dear to me on earth. . . . He has blessed wonderfully in the trial. . . . I never felt Him so near as these past days.'

So it is always! When the Lord afflicts, He pours in the balm of comfort, and brings blessing out of the experience.

When famine came to the West Nile District of Uganda in 1918, John Buyse, together with others, went there and helped to distribute famine relief supplied by the British Government. He could be seen at the head of a line of a hundred porters carrying food to the stricken people. It was as a result of this ministry that work was opened in that area.

Uncle John's eyes were always on the unreached parts. Far from confining his attention to the work around Ara, he opened work to the north of that area. He sent out many of his converts as evangelists, and through their instrumentality the Gospel was preached over a wide area. Many of those sent out by him continued in the work until old age.

His long safaris to and in French territory are recorded later. Having got the work there under way, he returned to Congo, and before long went on furlough. He spent it in America, but on his way there he visited his native Holland again, to the joy of his parents and other members of the family.

When he made his way back to Africa in 1928, he was met in Kenya by Mabel Easton and they were united in marriage at Kijabe. Mabel had already seen some years of service in Congo, having gone to the field in 1918. She was a teacher and had worked at Dungu among the Azandes. She had the pen of a ready writer and some of the articles she wrote are gems of missionary literature.

They were stationed at Kasengu for some time, but later worked at Aru in the Lugbara tribe for a number of years.

Their characters were complementary. John was typically Dutch, with a strength of serious conviction. Mabel had a humorous way of tempering his sometimes outspoken opinions, and smoothing over situations created by his rugged bluntness of speech.

On one of his furloughs in America, John learned how to fill teeth so that when he returned to the field he was able to help missionaries and others along this line.

Twice he became Acting Field Director while Mr. Van Dusen was on furlough. On one occasion at a missionary conference he gave vent forcibly to his convictions as to the role of women in missionary work, and spoke of

stations where 'the woman wears the overalls'. Next time
the missionaries met in conference they were amused to
find on the notice board a photo placed there by Mabel
showing John in well-patched overalls, with the caption
'Overalls over'auled'!

But in spite of his naturally rigid outlook, Uncle John
was very gracious and was loved by all. He had a deeply
spiritual influence and constantly sought to strengthen
both African Christians and missionaries in their faith.

After years of safari on foot and cycle, they at last
secured a second-hand car. Mabel promptly named it
'Micah' (My car). How Uncle John enjoyed driving it! It
did good service transporting evangelists to their posts,
taking the sick to hospital, carrying workmen out to the
bush to cut poles for building or wood to burn the bricks
they had made. He never lost his love of the sea, and it was
said that in the wet season he would drive straight through
the huge puddles just to hear the splash of the water!

He was loved by the M.K.s—which, being interpreted,
stands for 'missionary kids', the children of the missionaries. At the beginning of the term at Rethy Academy he
would take a carload of them to school. In the early days
of the Mission it was a rule that all missionaries must take
a rest after the midday meal. With most of the older missionaries this became a habit which it was difficult to
break. In the course of the journey, after they had had
their picnic lunch, Uncle John would draw the car to the
side of the road, lean over the steering wheel and have his
siesta. The children would laugh and joke, and play with
the hairs on his arms; but it took more than that to rouse
him before his ten or fifteen minutes had elapsed. During
the course of the term, each of the children would be
called to sit in his dental chair to have their teeth examined
and attended to.

Later he and Mabel were stationed at Goli, still among

the Alurs, but on the other side of the international boundary, in the West Nile District of Uganda. But ever the unreached parts called him, and he was burdened for those who had never heard the emancipating message. The story of his work in the Southern Sudan must await a later chapter.

19

Education

IN Congo as in all the other fields, schools were opened in the early days. The preaching of the Gospel brought in its train the need that converts and enquirers should be taught to read the Word of God for themselves, either in the vernaculars or in linguae francae.

Gradually the primitive classes, often held on the veranda of the missionary's house, or under a spreading tree, developed into more organized schools, erstwhile pupils being the teachers; but it was all very elementary.

The Catholic Missions, however, were providing better and more advanced education. They were in a position to do so, for in 1926 an agreement was made between the State and the Vatican that all subsidies for education should be given to Roman Catholic Missions. The generous grants made it possible for thousands of Congolese to be given primary education in Catholic schools and for large establishments of higher education to be erected. Protestant Missions did their best, but funds were insufficient; nor was it felt that money given for evangelization should be used for a purpose which was primarily the responsibility of the Government.

For the A.I.M. the problem was not entirely resolved when, in 1948, the Government modified its policy and agreed to subsidize all education which met their requirements. Many of the missionaries as well as supporters at home were of the opinion that the Mission should not become involved in the State education programme but confine itself to evangelism and Bible teaching. A deep division of opinion was revealed when the question was discussed at Field Conferences. The only solution to the impasse lay in prayer, and a number of the missionaries sought the Lord's face very earnestly that He would show His will clearly. When therefore the Conference met again, the vote in favour of taking government subsidies was almost unanimous.

Although the Mission strained every nerve to make up the lost ground, the progress made came far short of meeting the situation, or the aspirations of the Africans. Some primary schools were already up to government standard. Others were brought up to the required level, teachers being provided by those who had graduated from a low-level teacher-training school already in existence. These were able to take their places in the schools as long as the principal had the required qualifications. At that time only missionaries who had taken a course in Belgium were thus qualified.

Further handicaps were due to the fact that the subsidies given by the Government only covered a percentage of the cost of the buildings, or of equipment and supplies. And even this was only refunded months after the expenses had been met by the Missions. This meant that the Mission had to find large sums of money if the government standard was to be maintained, only a proportion of which was eventually repaid. Nor would the State allow fees to be charged.

A Teacher Training College (Ecole de Moniteurs) on the secondary level was opened at Aungba. It was only possible to erect the necessary buildings by the energy of Earl Dix, a missionary-builder who had the confidence of the Africans and was able to get the best out of them, and also to get supplies in bulk at a considerably lower rate than usual. The course at the school was one of four years, taught entirely in French. Only a few graduated annually from it. The disturbances in the years following the attainment of independence interrupted the teacher-training programme; but it has now been resumed.

Schools, however, even the most elementary, presuppose reading matter. This entails translation. In the Congo field, as in all others, much has been done to overcome the curse of Babel. Before the knowledge of the trade languages had spread, many missionaries, in addition to other work, did their best to learn the language of the tribe in which they were working and to translate portions of the Scriptures. Perseverance and patience resulted in this being achieved in Azande, Logo, Kakwa, Lugbara, Lendu and other tongues. Later, however, it was found advisable to follow the example of Government and concentrate on linguae francae. Thus the A.I.M. territory divided itself into three language areas—Azande in the north, Bangala in the centre and Kingwana in the south. Devoted workers gave time and mental sweat to these languages and enlisted the co-operation of other missions working in the same tongues. Together they produced the Bangala New Testament, which was warmly welcomed. When the books arrived from the British and Foreign Bible Society, Africans walked many miles to buy them and thousands were disposed of. The whole Bible followed some years later, the translation of the New Testament being revised at the same time. This also was very popular.

Bangala is a very simple language, if indeed it is worthy of the name of language at all. Unlike the vernaculars, its vocabulary is limited as is also its grammar. It is, however, easy to read, and even though the translation is at times ambiguous, sales have mounted and its popularity has been maintained over many years. Moreover, God has used it and by reading it many have come to the Lord and have been built up in their most holy faith.

Work was also done in Kingwana. The New Testament was published in that language. Kingwana is a kind of degenerate Swahili. It was felt by many that it should be improved and approximate more closely to its mother language so that readers might be able to take advantage of the extensive literature in it. A committee on which the A.I.M. was represented worked on this. The New Testament was translated into Congo-Swahili and published. While its advanced form was not understood by the ordinary peasant, it was introduced into the schools and spread rapidly. Work has since been done on the Old Testament, but again the serious interruptions which have occurred since Independence have hindered the work. However, the Union Version of the Scriptures in East African Swahili is now being used by the more advanced Congolese.

As regards Azande, John, Mark and Luke were translated in early days, in co-operation with the missionaries of the Church Missionary Society working in Southern Sudan. These were followed by the whole of the New Testament in 1938 and the Psalms. For some years Joan Utting has been working on the translation of the Old Testament, helped by a number of Africans; but the task is Herculean, and has been hindered by the fact that Congo had to be evacuated on account of the disturbances. The British and Foreign Bible Society is providing welcome aid.

In addition to the Scriptures, school books and other reading matter have been produced in all these three languages.

We have already mentioned the Winsor family, four of whose members have served in Congo. Amy became the wife of Floyd Pierson; Dora married Mr. William Deans of the Immanuel Mission, working at Nyankunde, a station which had originally belonged to the A.I.M. Rachel became the wife of Paul Stough, and passed away in Congo in 1944. Earl, the only male member, came to Africa in 1926, and the matter of education there can hardly be mentioned without introducing his name. Before coming to the field he had been a Professor at Wheaton College, Illinois.

After teaching in the Evangelists' School at Aba for several years, Professor and Mrs. Winsor went to Rethy to organize Rethy Academy, the school for the children of missionaries, and Earl became its principal. Much of its outstanding success throughout the years has been due to the foundations laid by him.

Owing to the serious illness of his wife, Earl remained in America for some years after going on furlough in 1936, and resumed his work at Wheaton College. Following his wife's homecall in 1947, and as the educational side of the work in Congo assumed increasing importance, the missionaries called on him to return to become Director of Education. He arrived back on the field in 1949. The post, coupled with that of Legal Representative, entailed much hard work and the overcoming of many difficulties. Criticism and discouragement had to be faced, and this was hard to one of such a sensitive nature as his; but he placed the educational programme on a firm footing. He became the first principal of the Teacher Training College at Aungba, and the graduates not only gained sound academic training but also came out more firmly established in their faith. In 1958 he married Ada Rury, a friend of the family and of the Mission.

The unrest at the time of Independence brought a changed spirit among the Congolese, and many of the students showed little gratitude for the hard work and interest which he had expended to help them.

When the troubles in Congo necessitated their leaving, the Winsors went to assist at Kijabe.

There are many others whose names should be mentioned in connection with the educational work; but space will not permit. We cannot, however, pass by the names of Burnetta Wambold, who did so much to set the programme on its feet, and Martha Lohrmann who worked hard behind the scenes; of Fred Lasse who gained the necessary qualifications when past middle age, and taught in both the Teacher Training School at Blukwa, and later in the Monitors' School at Aungba; of Carl Becker Junior who became the Director of Education after Mr. Winsor. By great patience and wise counsel Carl prepared Mr. Rafael Etsea so that when the responsibility for education was put into the hands of the African church, he was able to take that leading position.

20

Medical

As all the fields of the A.I.M., Congo owes much to its medical work.

The first hospital was opened at Aba by Dr. Elizabeth Morse Hurlburt. When she passed away in 1922, it was left without a resident doctor until 1926, when Dr. and Mrs. Ralph Kleinschmidt, who had served in Congo since 1923 under another Mission, transferred to the A.I.M. Although they were posted to other stations for brief periods during their early years, their life-work was centred at Aba. 'Centred'—for they covered a large field. The treatment of leprosy and supervision of widely separated colonies, not only in A.I.M. areas but also in those of other missions in north-east Congo, was the main task which occupied them until Doctor's homecall in 1964. They gave the work its character and name.

Ralph Kleinschmidt had come to the Lord at the early age of five. As he grew up he maintained a bright testimony. It was during his period of internship in a large hospital that he came into contact with a supervisor of nurses. His moral standards stood out in such marked contrast to that of others that she was impressed. He was able to lead her to the Lord. Later they married and eventually he and Coralee went to Africa together.

The doctor was a humble, gracious man who was beloved by all. Amid the demands made upon him, by night or day, travelling on foot, or bicycle or motor-car, he was always ready to point his patients to the Great Physician.

On one occasion a woman suffering from leprosy gave this testimony :

> 'Thanks to God for this leprosy ! Had I not contracted this disease, I never would have heard about Jesus Who is the Great Doctor who cleanses the leprosy of my heart. This Dr. Kleinschmidt treats me for the leprosy in my body, but he also tells me of the Great Physician who cures the leprosy of sin. One of these days, I'll be with this Heavenly Physician and receive a new body. Thanks for this leprosy which has brought me to this place of God.'

At the time of his death, Doctor had nearly three thousand patients under his care in the various colonies. Thanks to the new drugs, many had been discharged, the disease having been arrested. There were periods during his service on the field when he was the only doctor in an area of approximately 200,000 square miles.

Coralee was a most efficient nurse and there are few of the missionaries who have not profited from the kindly and diligent ministry of this couple in times of need. Many babies whom they ushered into the world are now serving as missionaries. Nor would the story be complete without the mention of Mary White, the nurse who served so faithfully during almost the whole time of their service at Aba.

The Kleinschmidts left for their first furlough in 1932. It was providential that just at that time Dr. and Mrs. Carl K. Becker—who also had served for a short time with another Congo Mission—transferred to the A.I.M. and entered into the work at Aba Hospital. Before responding to the call to missionary service, Dr. Becker had

had a large practice in Boyertown, Philadelphia.

When the Kleinschmidts returned from furlough, Dr. and Mrs. Becker were assigned to Rethy for a time, but later went to open medical work at Oicha, in the pygmy forest, the most southerly station in the A.I.M. field. The work there had only recently been commenced. Here he started from scratch, and gradually built up a very large hospital. His reputation as a doctor and surgeon spread far and wide, and after a few years many European and African patients travelled hundreds of miles to consult him. Building after building was added to the primitive hut in which he started, until a widely spread and well-equipped hospital came into being. Dr. Becker, like Dr. Kleinschmidt, took an interest in leprosy, and did valuable research into that disease. A colony which, at one time, housed about four thousand patients was established at Oicha. As the years went by, the Gospel seed brought forth fruit abundantly in that place and a church was formed of which pastor, officers and members were all people who suffered from leprosy. It was a strong church, and its liberality exceeded that of many others.

When at Aba, Dr. Becker had commenced classes for training African dressers. These were continued by Dr. Kleinschmidt after his return from furlough. Going to Oicha, Dr. Becker started classes there also. Later the trainees were able to take the State Examinations for 'Aide-Infirmiers'. This was the lowest possible medical qualification, but they were well and thoroughly trained. They went out to work in dispensaries on nearly every station of the Mission. Every month or six weeks, they were visited by a doctor. Medicines were standardized and these men did excellent work. Courses for girls were added later. For the most part these Africans were dedicated Christians, who were conscious of a call from God for the work. They not only gave help to ailing bodies but also preached the Gospel to the crowds who attended and gave words of comfort to those who sorrowed.

Dr. Becker fully practises the maxim laid down by Dr. Nina Maynard of Kola Ndoto: 'Never do anything which an African can be trained to do.' As soon as a national could take responsibility, it was given to him. While patient with their shortcomings, he expects a high standard from his helpers, and they usually measure up to it.

For the greater part of the time he had no other doctor with him. Then Dr. Wilcke joined him for a while. After that Dr. Herbert Atkinson worked with him, and Dr. Wilcke went to take charge of the hospital at Rethy. The work increased year by year, until nearly two thousand outpatients were dealt with daily. The straightforward cases could be given treatment by the Africans he had trained. The more serious illnesses were referred to the missionary nurses who worked so loyally with him. Cases beyond their ability were taken to the doctor himself. Dr. Becker insisted that all cases should be properly examined and diagnosed. He was never satisfied until he had discovered the root of the trouble.

He operated regularly about four afternoons a week, as well as emergencies by night and day, visited the huge leper settlement, rarely missed the daily prayer meeting or the church services on Sundays or week-nights, held prayer meetings and Bible classes with his dressers, took part in evangelistic services among the patients and made regular medical trips to other stations.

Such activity would have been impossible were it not for the faithful co-operation of the missionary nurses who gave themselves unsparingly to the work. Without the help of Jewel Olson, Vera Thiessen, Mary Heyward and others, Dr. Becker would have been greatly handicapped. Special mention must be made of one who worked for many years at Aba and then came to Oicha to work with

Dr. Becker—Edna Amstutz, who served actively until late in life. Only the disturbances in Congo made her eventually leave her post.

As if such a heaped-up life were not sufficient for a man who, by this time, was nearing 'threescore years and ten', the post of Field Director was added when Bwana Van laid it down. Dr. Becker was such an outstanding leader that only he could command the confidence of the missionaries.

Yet with this over-busy programme, Dr. Becker never appeared to be hurried or impatient. He kept up to date not only in professional reading but in spiritual matters also. He always seemed to have read the latest books. Regular as clockwork, Dr. Becker left his house at his set hour in the early morning to start his day at the hospital, having already had his time of communion with His Lord over the Word, and often having been called in the night to attend to an accident case or perform an emergency operation. He never took a holiday if he could help it. When he went on furlough, he returned to the work to which he was dedicated after two or three months. On one occasion he flew home to America for emergency surgery himself; three months later he was back at his post again.

'How do you do it, Dr. Becker?' I once asked him when we were travelling together, referring to the amount of work he got through.

'By filling in the chinks,' he replied. And he referred to a statement by Oswald Sanders:

'When we have comparatively little to carry in the case, it seems as full as when we have much, because the less we have the more carelessly we pack it. The man who claims to have no time is most likely guilty of "careless packing".'

Both Dr. and Mrs. Becker are deeply loved by missionaries and Africans alike. She has been a loyal helpmeet, constantly busy in the hospital, and with a heavy burden of entertaining the many guests who came to visit the doctor or see the work which became so well known. Even when crippled with arthritis, she still spends a large part of her time dispensing medicines and doing other jobs.

They are still carrying on. During the disturbances which followed on the granting of Independence, they remained at their post. Only when that part of the country was overrun by the rebels did they leave, to return at the first opportunity.

The hospital at Rethy was opened by Dr. Lewis Trout in the late 1920s. For many years after he left, the work was without a resident doctor. It was eventually manned by Dr. and Mrs. Wilcke.

After the disturbances, an evangelical medical centre on a co-operative basis was opened at Nyankunde, south of Bunia. Dr. Becker is in charge, and the staff consists of half-a-dozen doctors, as well as nurses, from A.I.M. and other like-minded missions. In addition to a hospital accommodating many in-patients and a colossal out-patient clinic, there is a training school for African assistants. Radio contact is maintained with all A.I.M. stations in Congo, and the M.A.F. plane makes it possible for the doctors to supervise station dispensaries as well as to deal with emergencies. No doctors are now resident at Oicha, Rethy and Aba, which, with their dependent dispensaries, are run by nurses with African helpers.

There is another hospital at Banda, among the Azande. Here Dr. Paul Brown has a busy schedule of operations, in which he is assisted by his wife and another nurse.

21

The Church Develops

THE first Evangelists' School was opened at Aba in 1924 in the care of Mr. and Mrs. Harry Stam. Candidates from all over the Congo field gathered there. Many of those who were in the first class are now leaders in the work. After many years at Aba, this school was transferred to Adi, and a Pastors' Course was added to its curriculum. Later another Evangelists' School was opened at Linga to cater particularly for candidates from the southern part of the field. In more recent years one was opened at Napopo for the training of Azande evangelists.

The Pastors' Course at Adi served the whole field and provided two further years of training beyond that of the Evangelists' School. All these classes were necessarily on a very low level. The evangelists who desired to take advantage of them had had only two or three years of primary education and were quite unused to study. It was hard and discouraging work for the teachers. Even when, about 1948, the Pastors' Course was started, the poor educational background, combined with chronic bilharzia or malaria which sapped their energy, made it necessary to teach very simply and progress slowly. The Rev. Peter Brashler was responsible for this course until, in 1963, he was called to succeed Dr. Becker as Field Director. The Lord honoured the teaching, and those who followed it obtained a good grounding in the Word of God. Peter Stam, who later became Home Director in Canada, was on the staff.

There are many others who have served long and faithfully in the Congo; but space will not permit more than a brief mention of a few of them.

Mr. and Mrs. A. P. Uhlinger went to the field in 1917. At that time they wrote:

'When the Lord Jesus comes to receive His redeemed ones unto Himself, we would like to be in Africa.'

Apart from furloughs, they remained in Congo until the disturbances of 1964 forced all our missionaries to withdraw. They were then well past the allotted span. They had faithfully ministered to churches in the southern half of the field, spoke several languages, and Mrs. Uhlinger became an authority in Kingwana.

Olive Love gave herself to girls' work. She built up large homes for them first at Bogoro and then at Blukwa. She also gathered around her a considerable family of orphans in the latter place. No sacrifice was too great for her to make for those in her care. She went to the field in 1924 and is still there as we write.

Among the British workers not yet mentioned are two ladies who rendered long and faithful service. Sarah Stirton went to Congo in 1912. She was a nurse and worked among the Alur tribe at Kasengu and Ara. When little was done for the helpless and hopeless sufferers from sleeping sickness she ministered to them and pointed them to Christ. Floyd Pierson told me that he would think it well worth all the hardships and deprivations of coming to Africa if he could have people looking up into his eyes with the same gaze of love and appreciation they gave to Sarah Stirton. Health forced her to retire in 1939, but she spent herself in encouraging circles of prayer helpers in the Merseyside area until she passed away in 1956.

Ethel Wightman went to the field in 1922. Two sisters, Florence and Lucy McCord, had gone out from Ireland, but Florence had passed away after a short time on the field. Ethel Wightman heard the call for someone to fill the vacant place. She and Lucy worked among the Logo together as sisters until Lucy passed away in 1940. The girls owe much to her care and prayers. Having been trained at the Missionary School of Medicine in London, she was recognized by the State as a medical worker. She had a busy dispensary and carried the patients on her heart. She also supervised a leper colony.

There are others too who spent long years in Congo. Mr. and Mrs. Harter and Miss Myrtle Wilson came out together in 1917, and were in the party which was shipwrecked off Cape Town. The Harters worked faithfully in the southern part of the field. Myrtle Wilson (Missi Mertelli) was sent to Dungu on a temporary assignment, and stayed there for forty years! There was Jack Litchman, the converted Hebrew who worked laboriously in the Rethy–Linga district for a similar period. He also was a medical worker, having taken the prescribed course in Belgium. He used this as he travelled round the area preaching the Gospel and encouraging the evangelists. Nor can we pass by Rose Mary Hayes. She went to Congo in middle life, and served at Aba until she was nearly ninety years of age. She learned the Mondo language, and was probably the only European who could speak it. As long as she was able she travelled among that tribe preaching the Gospel.

An interesting variation from ordinary missionary activity was inaugurated when Austin Paul started a music school. He originally began to train a band of horn-players to assist in the evangelistic campaigns which he held all over the Congo field. It became so popular that he made it into a school and each of the Congo churches sent pupils to learn how to play wind instruments. While on furlough in America he had received gifts of second-hand cornets and trombones which he used in his classes. With the assistance of Mrs. Paul he taught the pupils staff notation, and gradually the weird sound which emanated from his classrooms evolved into well-known hymns. Before long the singing in every station church and many of the out-churches was led by cornets or trombones. The school was very successful. The average standard of playing was good, and some of the students turned out to be excellent. Austin Paul's zeal for evangelism spread to his pupils, and many people attribute their conversion to him and to his evangelistic teams.

Austin Paul went to the field as a young man in 1923 and in spite, latterly, of poor health and at least one major operation, he continued for over forty years. In 1926 he married Betty Rieman who had gone to the field the year before he. She proved a very loyal wife to whom he owed much. Her quiet and patient demeanour endeared her to all. She brought up her children wisely and lovingly, and all are now engaged in the Lord's service, at home or overseas. One daughter is the wife of Dr. Herbert Atkinson of Oicha. A son is also serving in Congo as an associate missionary.

When the Stauffachers felt that the time had come to retire from active missionary service, they came to Congo, where their two sons, Raymond and Claudon, were serving. They settled at Ruwenzori (Mwenda) on the foothills of the Mountains of the Moon, not far from the spot where John had first crossed the Semliki into Congo. There they dedicated themselves to a ministry to missionaries who could have restful holidays in the cool and quiet of that station. Many found refreshment for body and soul there.

Gradually, however, John's strength declined until, at length they decided to go to Kenya for medical attention. He passed away at Kijabe in 1944.

Florence Stauffacher returned to Congo, spending the remainder of her days with her son Claudon and his wife at Mwenda and Oicha.

Not the least interesting work in Congo is that among the pygmies. These quaint little people live in the depths of the Ituri Forest. They stand between 3 and 5 feet high. Their houses are made from saplings covered with leaves, and since they do not remain long in any one neighbourhood, it is of little importance that the huts are short-lived. The women are the builders.

The pygmies are constantly on the move, staying in one locality while hunting animals there, and then moving on. As hunters they are amazing, understanding the ways of wild animals perfectly. They are dead shots with their diminutive bows and arrows and fearless as they attack even elephants and buffaloes with their spears.

Their clothing is bark-cloth. A piece of bark is stripped from a certain kind of tree and pounded with an ivory hammer until they have a piece about 30 inches wide and a yard long. This is worn as a loin-cloth.

Each group of pygmies is attached to a clan of another forest tribe, who are known as their 'overlords'. These overlords help them with weapons for the hunt and exercise a kind of beneficent paternalism over them. Since the pygmies do not normally dig gardens, they obtain their supplies of garden produce from their overlords in exchange for meat.

Restless and nomadic, these people are not easy to reach with the Gospel. Mr. and Mrs. Jim Bell and Margaret Clapper with African helpers devoted themselves to this task. As a result, the Gospel story, with hymns and choruses, has become widely known among them. Many have professed conversion, and in some cases the reality of the experience has shown itself in changed lives. A few have confessed Christ in baptism, and a number of pygmy churches have been erected.

This is not the place to enter with any detail into the troubles which have come to north-east Congo.

Suddenly, on 30th June 1960, the Independence for which the country had been so inadequately prepared was granted. Yet, under the leading of the Holy Spirit, the church had been prepared. The new church constitution gave absolute autonomy and the Church Councils which were established were composed entirely of Africans.

Shortly after the critical date, anti-white troubles arose and on the advice of the respective consuls, many of the missionaries crossed into Uganda. But things quietened down quickly, and they were able to return. In January 1961, however, things took a more serious turn, and again the consular authorities urged missionaries to move out of Congo. Most of them did so after frustrating and irritating delays. Yet again, after a few months things settled down and the missionaries returned and resumed their work.

But a much more serious interruption occurred in 1964. There was a rebel movement organized by leaders who had gone to China for special training. The greater part of the population of north-east Congo, disillusioned at the failure of the Government to fulfil the glowing promises of prosperity as the accompaniments of Independence, easily swung over to the rebel cause. Stanleyville fell to them in August, and they proceeded to advance over the whole of the north-east province, killing government officials and all in positions of responsibility or leadership. Many Europeans were arrested and maltreated, and some killed.

Again the Consuls urged the missionaries to leave. Peter

Brashler, the Field Director of Congo, had foreseen the trouble and went to Bunia, the administrative centre, in an attempt to get permits for the missionaries to leave the country. But the necessary forms were out of stock. Peter borrowed the one which was left, hurried back the 120 miles to Rethy, had a supply of forms printed and rushed back with them the next day. He stood over each of the four officials whose signatures and seals were necessary to authenticate the documents. When all was satisfactorily completed, he returned to Rethy, ready for the orders to evacuate.

The A.I.M. stations being, for the most part, close to the borders with Uganda, Central African Republic or Sudan, all our missionaries were able to leave, although all suffered inconvenience and insult, and some had difficult experiences. One couple, Rev. and Mrs. Charles Davis, new missionaries, were teaching at the Theological Seminary at Banjwadi, a station of the Unevangelized Fields Mission, near Stanleyville. They were unable to get away and suffered more than others. But eventually they were flown out of Stanleyville. Other Missions—Unevangelized Fields Mission, Worldwide Evangelization Crusade and Yakusu, the most easterly station of the Baptist Missionary Society—were cut off, their cars were confiscated and they were stranded. Eventually some of their missionaries suffered martyrdom.

The missionaries who left could take practically nothing with them, and their homes and possessions left behind were looted and destroyed.

The rebels also sought for church leaders. In the mercy of God, none of our pastors lost their lives. Some fled the country for a time, others hid in the long grass for months on end, returning to their posts when conditions improved. Some were tortured. A few of the leading Christians were killed.

Once again, however, God brought about the unexpected. The rebels were gradually driven back, the people turned against them and calm reigned once more. In 1966 missionaries returned to receive a royal welcome not only from their adherents but from all. They found that the experiences had brought rich blessing to the churches. The work had gone on in the hands of the pastors and evangelists. The troubled conditions had driven many to seek the Lord, and backsliders and those whose devotion had grown cold came back with repentance and renewed zeal. Large numbers had been baptized after careful examination, and the whole tempo of the life of the church had been quickened.

PART FIVE

WEST NILE DISTRICT, UGANDA

Reaping in the Forgotten Corner

22

Out of Weakness Made Strong

THE doctor examined the thin, small-built lad who came before him. Solemnly he percussed his chest and listened to it with his stethoscope. At last he gave his diagnosis. The cough which had been so troublesome of late, aggravated by the tea dust in his place of business, sprang from a tuberculous spot on his lung. He must go away to a sanatorium for treatment.

Life is very sweet at nineteen, and it seemed to Albert E. Vollor that this meant the end of all his hopes for a life of active usefulness in the Lord's service.

He had been born in south-east London. His parents were influenced by the preaching of the well-known C. H. Spurgeon, but they never became committed Christians. However, at the age of three he was taken by his sister to a local Sunday School. When he was about twelve years old he joined the Boys' Brigade and attended the Bible Class. Shortly afterwards a London City Missionary handed him a tract entitled 'Salvation for the chief of sinners' which was the means of his conversion. The Boys' Brigade had lost many of its officers, and before long he and another young fellow took a leading part.

He joined the local church and became a teacher in the Sunday School. This was very profitable, for he had to study in order to teach. He also joined the Scripture Union and read steadily through the Scriptures.

He had taken his first job when he was seven, earning the princely salary of three shillings a week by working after school hours. But a law was passed forbidding the employment of children under the age of eleven; so being then only nine, he had to leave. School life ended when he was thirteen, and he went to work for a tea firm.

Living in the locality, he became interested in the Cambridge University Mission's club in Bermondsey and joined other Christians there. A missionary band was formed called 'The Praying Out Band' in which the members, after declaring their faith in Christ as Saviour, stated that they would go abroad as missionaries unless God prevented. It was a seed-bed for missionaries. Fred Morris and Jack Batstone had already joined the ranks of the A.I.M. Fred Laverick followed later. Paul Gibson went to the Church Missionary Society as did Eddie Phillips. Vivian Donnithorne went to China, and Bert Jackson to Ruanda. Bert Vollor was full of hopeful anticipation of foreign service.

When, therefore, T.B. of the lung was diagnosed, it seemed the death knell of all his hopes. But the Praying Out Band would not accept this, and joined together to pray him through. He spent some months in the sanatorium. When he was discharged, he worked as a cashier for a well-known biscuit firm.

By this time, the First World War had started, and young fellows rushed to join the army. After the heavy losses of the early years, conscription was introduced, and Bert Vollor was called up. He presented himself at the recruiting office, but when given a medical examination, he was rejected as unfit.

Nothing daunted, 'being strong in faith', he went forward to prepare himself for the Lord's service. Through the help of friends, and bursaries, he was able to go to

Queens' College, Cambridge. He studied there for three years. His third year was an outstanding one in his life, for in it he gained his B.A. degree (later M.A.), got married and was ordained in the Anglican Church, and he and his wife offered to the A.I.M. They were accepted. He served for two years as a curate at Christchurch, Spitalfields, and they sailed for the West Nile District of Uganda in 1923.

Before applying to the A.I.M., Bert Vollor had carefully studied the Faith Basis of the Mission. He was appalled by appeals made by some Societies saying that unless money was given the work of God would cease. It was one of the means which God used to lead him to offer to the Mission. In later years, he issued the following statement:

'In circulating this testimony to God's faithfulness, I would like it to be understood that it has no other purpose but the glory of our Heavenly Father and for the encouragement of any who find Matthew 6 : 33 difficult.
                                                        A. E. Vollor

'No one in a Mission on the "Faith Basis" accuses missionaries in other societies of lack of faith in God. Yet when one has felt the call to look to God alone for anything, then there is a sense of privilege. Matthew 6:33 brings a precious promise from our gracious and all-powerful Heavenly Father.

'God certainly called men like George Muller and Peter C. Scott to great faith in avoiding appeals to men, but looking only to God for the necessary supplies to carry on the work which God had given them to do.

'Not all on the Faith Basis are called individually as they were. Yet all who are called to join the A.I.M. must have had a call to a special exercise of faith in God for their daily needs and for the support of their work, though not all in the same way or to the same degree, and it is usually only after experience on the field that one realizes the wonder of God's keeping power and the joyful realization that our Father draws His children ever nearer to Him.

'Personally there was a time when I felt that the way some pleading appeals for money for the Lord's work were worded was dishonouring to God. It was the time when the Lord was calling me to missionary work and it was part of the Lord's call to me to join the A.I.M.

'How the Faith Basis would work out I did not know.

'The Bishop to whom I applied for ordination said, in effect, "If this fellow likes to take his life in his hands and go unsupported into the wilds of Africa, let him; but he has a responsibility to his wife and ought not to lead her into such a situation." I liked what the Bishop said because there was a lot of common sense in it and because, moreover, he was a bachelor. Nevertheless, neither of us had any doubt that the Lord was calling us and the responsibility was His.

'After we had applied to the Council of the A.I.M. a lady from another part of London, whom I had never met, and who only knew us as missionary candidates, felt called of God to sell out some shares and so provided what was needed for our fares to Africa. We were not in a position to know the full cost of the fare to Arua nor that we lacked a considerable amount. During the farewell in London we were handed an envelope containing £50 which was in fact a loving provision from above. We reached Arua safely, the Lord supplying all our needs, as He has from that day to this. His promises, as in Phil. 4 : 19, are literally fulfilled.

'After some years on the field our minds were not on furlough till we received a telegram—"Fare and home provided, arrange furlough." Someone in Australia whose identity has never been revealed to us had been moved of God to provide the fare, and a servant of God at home had been led of God to prepare a cottage fully furnished for missionaries' use. We are constrained to give thanks to our God.

'(I can add more to this incident. My wife and I were on furlough and together with Miss Utting, were ready to return to the field. After prayer, passages had been reserved in faith, although funds were not yet in hand. The time for sailing drew near, and still the money had not come. The Council called us in and said that unless the funds came in by the following Tuesday—the date of the Annual Meeting in London—the passages would have to be relinquished. On that very morning, a letter posted many weeks before in Australia reached the Chairman of the Council containing a draft to be applied to anything lacking for the return of the Richardsons and Miss Utting to the field, the balance to be applied to the homecoming expenses of the Vollors!)

'So it has been, though in a different way, on each occasion when furlough time has come round. Once it was a large gift by one who had expected to travel to Africa herself but was detained at home. At another time a plain envelope was dropped into the letter-box of the London Office during the lunch hour, and the secretary, on his return, found it contained £100 for the Vollors' return to the field.

'In many ways through the years our God has proved that He is able to make all grace abound to His own. The Lord has ever been faithful and delights in surprising us with His ways of love.

'There were times when money was short, but we never lacked. We were able to send our three children to school. The boy went to Monkton Combe and the fees and the cost of equipment etc. in England seemed to be a large figure compared with our field income; but the Lord met every need, as He did when the girls likewise returned to England for schooling and in the days when (unlike the present) the parents paid quite a big bill for their children in Teacher Training College.

'From the year 1928 when British missionaries began to be paid from British sources alone, I believe I am right in saying that they have received 100% allowances these 34 years (written in 1962). During that time the rate of allowances has been increased on several occasions and this last year finished up with a bonus on top of the 100%. Have we not a faithful God?

'In the course of our missionary work we have had help from Government grants for which we give thanks to God. Yet, though the Government may seem rich and powerful, there is nothing to compare with the wealth and power of our God, and it is a good thing to trust Him. He is with us all the day. Not only does He meet our personal financial needs and those of the work He has given us to do, but His promise of "All your needs" includes things spiritual and eternal, as well as those material and temporal. For this we give thanks and to Him we give continual praise.'

The West Nile District of Uganda to which the Vollors were appointed had been by-passed by the main stream of missionary endeavour. The whole of Uganda had been apportioned to the Church Missionary Society, but such had been the demands on their personnel that by 1918 they had not been able to enter the area to the west of the River Nile. This had originally formed part of the Belgian Congo but an exchange of territory was negotiated by which the West Nile District was handed over to Great Britain and the British gave up all claim to the west shores of Lake Albert. The boundary between Congo and

Uganda in this area is somewhat unnatural, since it divides tribes so that part is in Congo and part in Uganda.

The entrance of the A.I.M. into this area had been almost accidental, yet it was divinely overruled. In 1918 the whole of the district was smitten with famine. At the same time a party of missionaries bound for Congo had been held up by the severe illness of one of their number. They encamped at Vurra, near the Congo border. The District Commissioner, Mr. Arthur Weatherhead, asked for the help of the Mission in administering famine relief. So it came about that the attention of the A.I.M. was drawn to the needs there. An agreement was entered into with the C.M.S. under which the A.I.M. would assume responsibility for the evangelization of this area, developing the work along Anglican lines, while adhering to evangelical tradition and faith basis.

A site was granted on a rise near the township of Arua, and here, while helping in famine relief, the first steps were taken towards building a mission station. Mr. and Mrs. Frank Gardner were among the earliest there. His brother, Alfred, also assisted for a time. Primitive mud huts were erected and first attempts were made to learn the Lugbara language. Repeated attacks of blackwater fever meant that the Gardners had to leave before long. But others came to help. The names of Mount, Crowell, John Buyse, Jim Bell are associated with those early days. Later Fred Morris went there.

The Vollors with their baby landed at Mombasa, and gradually made their way to Kampala in Uganda. From thence they journeyed to Butiaba and took the boat on Lake Albert. It only went as far as Pakwach. The remainder of their journey to Arua had to be made on foot, their goods carried on the heads of sturdy African porters.

23

The Mustard Seed Grows

ARRIVING at Arua, Mr. Vollor was appointed pastor and schoolmaster. They seemed grandiose titles, for the church consisted of twenty-six members who had been baptized the year before; and the school consisted of one class only, all over twenty years of age, and for just one hour daily they struggled with the Herculean task of learning to read and write. There were half a dozen who had already mastered the art, and they were being prepared to help teach others, although by no stretch of imagination could they be given the honourable title of 'teacher'.

So this young couple took over the work. Nobody could realize at that time the amount of grit, determination and energy contained in those diminutive bodies. When Bwana Hurlburt paid his first visit to them, he saw a very small person in front of the hut in which they were then living. He asked her:

'My dear, is your mother anywhere about?'

He was surprised and apologetic when Mrs. Vollor informed him who she was!

They soon got down to work. Mrs. Vollor began teaching the women, and together they endeavoured to organize the schools along better lines. The following year, however, the Education Department of the Government came into being and they followed the official curriculum.

So the schools have gone forward until today there is a fully organized educational system of primary, junior secondary, senior secondary schools and teacher-training college. All education, however, has now been taken over by the Government.

When the Mission started work, the people were very primitive and had no appreciation of the Gospel message, although it was preached with great earnestness by African evangelists. For six years the tribe was almost completely unresponsive.

About a year after the arrival of the Vollors, however, there was a great movement of the Spirit of God. One of the evangelists had gathered a few adherents round him. But his flock melted away when they took it into their heads to go to Kampala for work. However, a Lugbara villager asked him to go and preach to his people. This he did and almost immediately people crowded around him to be taught. Before long he had about one hundred who attended daily. Many came to the Lord. It soon spread to a larger area, and people in more distant villages asked for teachers. The only thing to do was to send out some of the new converts. Within twelve months there were many centres where there was daily Gospel teaching. Buildings were not available, and the teaching was usually given under trees. In course of time, these centres developed into organized churches. Every organized church had what it called 'Corners', places to which they sent members of the catechism class to teach the people to read. For Sunday services and Bible Classes they went to the church. These 'Corners' also became recognized churches in due course.

This movement in the villages was accompanied by parallel development on the mission station. Mary Quelch had recently joined them and as soon as she had learned something of the language, she was asked to start a Sunday

School. She called for volunteers and a number offered as teachers. But there were no scholars. So she told the teachers to go out into the villages and find their own classes. The first week they brought a few in. More came the second week. After that each week saw an increase and in a few months time there were eight hundred in attendance.

So the work grew both on the station and in the district. When one of the early missionaries translated the Gospel of Mark into Lugbara, there was an immediate desire to learn to read, and people crowded to the schools. Interest in the things of Christ spread rapidly.

But these were nearly all adults. They found it difficult to get in touch with the children. In fact, they were tempted to wonder whether there were any. The men used to deliver milk daily, and only after a long time did they begin to send their children. One day one of these lads fell from a tree and cut his leg. The houseboy brought him to Mrs. Vollor who applied some medicine and bound up his wound. This soon caught on, and the next day other boys brought milk and wanted medicine. Mrs. Vollor tied bandages on fingers and toes, legs and arms. This broke down the barrier and established friendly relations with them. Mrs. Morris started a Children's Service on Sunday. About a dozen children attended at first, all ready to flee at the first sign of danger. The service has continued ever since, and now about three hundred attend.

They wanted to start a Children's Service on Wednesday. So they gave balls to the boys in the highest class and sent them to the nearby villages to call the children in. The children came, played with the balls and then stayed for a Gospel service. These meetings were maintained for many years.

In the early years, the school term was three months long, and every fourth month was a holiday. Then Mr.

and Mrs. Vollor would pack their pots and pans, food and all that would be needed for themselves and their children and set off on safari to visit the Gospel centres which were springing up all over the place. They rose before daybreak, had breakfast and were off before the sun rose. The first centre was reached about eight o'clock. Notice had been sent in advance and the people were awaiting them. They would stay for an hour or two, testing the reading of Scripture, memory work and catechism, give a Gospel talk and then go farther on. In this way they visited two or three centres daily. The nights were spent at larger places, as they travelled throughout the district.

In the course of one of these safaris they noticed a young teenager teaching a row of people who were sitting on a fallen tree. They watched him for a while and were so impressed by his ability that they invited him to the mission station for further training. A class was started for such and in due course he went out as an evangelist. These Evangelists' Classes were commenced very early in the work, as soon as any desire was evinced to go out and carry the Gospel message to others. The people were unaccustomed to study and one term's teaching was all they could take in. Nowadays a three-year course is given as preparation for the work of evangelism.

Later two emerged from among the evangelists as leaders. They were appointed travelling superintendents to keep in touch with the various centres and the evangelists who were working in them. They were able to give good advice and help.

At that time there were no ordained pastors. Came a day when two who were earning salaries which were the envy of others, heard the call of God to give up their work and take up theological training. They were ordained in 1942, forerunners of nearly forty others who are now ministers of the Gospel in West Nile. Most of these have made large financial sacrifices on taking up this vocation.

On one occasion it was reported to Mr. Vollor that one of the schoolmasters, in charge of a school some 20 miles away, was demented. Mr. Vollor sent for him. A conversation indicated nothing abnormal, and he wondered what it was all about. So he said to him:

'Levi, you look rather thin. I think you should see a doctor.'

Levi looked into the eyes of his spiritual father and replied:

'I know people have been talking to you and saying that I am insane. Nothing of the kind! The thing is I'm very much concerned for the country to the north of us, the Mohammedan centres where there is no Christian witness at all, and I feel God is calling me to go up there. Because of this, people have told you that I am mad!'

So after they had prayed together about it, Levi rolled up a grass mat for a bed, took a few potatoes to eat on the way and set off alone. Mr. Vollor told him to come back at the end of a month and tell how he had fared.

When he returned he reported that he had travelled among the people there, had been well received and had found three centres where the people would be prepared to receive a resident evangelist. He had arrived back on a Thursday, and the Bible Class was about to commence. The matter was recounted to the Christians who attended, and volunteers were asked for. Three responded and went back with Levi.

A month later they came back and told of the opportunities and called for still more volunteers. By the end of two years, twenty-two centres had been opened in that Mohammedan area, and today most of these are organized churches. The work is still difficult, however, for the Mohammedans are in the majority and their influence is growing.

About 1926 Mrs. Vollor started cottage meetings for women. The Christian women on the station would go out to one or other of the areas around Arua. There they would gather the women together and have a meeting in one of the huts. Thus commenced a movement which has spread throughout the whole district and continues right up to the present.

In 1927 a women's prayer meeting was inaugurated. Mrs. Vollor arranged a prayer-cycle and sent it out quarterly with a letter to the existing centres. Today there are two hundred and fifty such centres where women lead a weekly prayer meeting. The prayer-cycle is still issued.

Mrs. Vollor also started conferences for women. Once a year they were invited to the station for four days of special teaching. In 1948, however, when nine hundred women attended, it was decided that each parish should organize its own. These are arranged by the local women who take complete charge. Missionaries only attend by invitation.

Some thirty years ago Mr. Vollor and the other missionaries realized that as long as they took the lead the Africans would never learn to carry responsibility. They therefore arranged that the work of the church should be directed by councils. At first a missionary took the chair, but later they placed the responsibility for leading and finding the money directly upon the Africans. After a while this was accepted. The Church was thus prepared for independence long before it came to the country as a whole, and has not had to pass through the turmoil which some churches have experienced. They regard the coming of independence to their country as presenting a challenge.

Mr. Vollor writes:

'All offices of the church are now held by Africans in the West Nile and they are entirely responsible for the work. The African clergy are humbly aware of the responsibilities of leadership and, while welcoming the continuing help of missionaries, are committing themselves in a new way to the Lord.'

It was a crowning reward for the faithful labours of Archdeacon Vollor when on Sunday, 7th June 1964, the first bishop from the A.I.M. West Nile was consecrated at St. Paul's Cathedral, Namirembe, Kampala. The Rev. Vollor had been given the Coronation Medal, had been decorated with the M.B.E., had been Archdeacon for some years, but he derived more satisfaction from the appointment of Silvano Wani as bishop than from all else.

He records:

'As we praise God for what He has wrought, we are startled to realize what has been accomplished in one generation. We remember the early stages in 1923 when, as a result of preaching the Gospel, only one group of twenty-two had been baptized. Now, only forty years later, thousands have been baptized, hundreds of churches are in existence and are in the care of ordained clergy, assisted by evangelists and lay readers, whom the Lord has called into His work. Amid the many changes in Africa today, let us pray the more earnestly for the African servants whom the Lord is raising up to be the shepherds of the flock.'

A more recent move has been the inauguration of 'Tentmakers'. These follow the example of St. Paul who, for a time, supported himself by tent-making while following his calling as a preacher of the Gospel. A number of qualified teachers have taken special training and have been ordained so that, while continuing to engage in educational work, they can serve as honorary pastors of local churches.

The Vollors retired in 1966, but his experience is still available to the Mission as he serves on the British Home Council.

24

Other Labourers

DESPITE war conditions which made sea-travel hazardous and passages difficult to obtain, the year 1941 saw notable additions to the staff of the West Nile District. Dr. and Mrs. E. H. Williams sailed in the first part of that year, and the Rev. and Mrs. Seton Maclure at its end.

'Ted' Williams was born in Kenya, his father having served under the Government there. He had been dedicated to God from his birth and had a desire to be a missionary even before his conversion at the age of thirteen. He took medical training at St. Bartholomew's Hospital. Later while serving at the Mildmay Mission Hospital he met a nurse who was training there. She too had been brought up by godly parents to whom she owed much.

Accepted by the Mission, they were married before sailing for Africa. Arriving in Arua, it was not long before they were busy on the station. Conditions were primitive in the extreme. Most new missionaries have to face a period of testing—usually along most unexpected lines—and the Williams were no exception. Whatever mental picture they had formed of missionary medical work, they were soon brought to earth with conditions at Arua. After training in up-to-date hospitals, they found themselves performing operations in a dusty room with nothing to protect them or the patients from the bits of grass which kept falling from the thatched roof, since there was no ceiling. It was thoroughly discouraging, especially as no money for hospital expenses arrived. They grew desperate and were strongly tempted to resign. But the Lord stepped in in the nick of time, and they were encouraged by two gifts. One was for the purchase of a second-hand car, the other was of £300 for a hospital building. Ted, practical as he is, set to work to build a little hospital. He left Muriel to see most of the outpatients, and he attended only to those who were seriously ill.

But experience showed that another site was needed. By this time there was a government hospital in Arua township, and with the development of education, the mission station was thronging with pupils. Also the Williams had seen the need for providing treatment for the hundreds of sufferers from leprosy in the area, and there was no room for the extension of the present site. A suitable place was found at Kuluva, about 7 miles west of Arua. In 1950 work was commenced there. Leprosy patients gathered, and Ted supervised the erection of the most necessary buildings.

By this time, Dr. Peter Williams had joined his brother, and a little later their parents came out also. They gave invaluable help. 'Grandpa' with his experience of building in East Africa was able to do many practical jobs. At the same time he developed his own original style of Flannel-graph, and was in great demand to address various meetings. 'Grannie' also was kept busy.

The work has expanded since those days, and staff has been augmented. Only for a short time have there been three doctors at Kuluva. For the greater part of the years, the burden has been carried by the two brothers, Peter specializing in ophthalmology. Peter also married a nurse. Other nurses joined the staff, two of them from Australia specially for leprosy work, supported by the Leprosy

Mission.

The African local government authority set apart a large area adjacent to Kuluva where those suffering from leprosy could live while receiving treatment. Only those suffering from the more contagious form of the disease came on to the station itself.

But in addition to the treatment of this and ordinary ailments, the two brothers find time for research. Ted has been busy trying to discover the incidence of malignancy and its relation to geographical and other factors, and how best to make use of cytotoxic drugs. Peter has undertaken research into the eye complications of onchoceriasis. Needless to say, all this would be impossible were it not for the loyal co-operation of the missionary nurses and the African dressers and helpers God has called to assist in the work.

However, whether treating eyes, or limbs or more general diseases, the main aim is ever spiritual. The body will die; the soul will live for ever, and only Christ can save it. The little church is often filled and in it many have found the Saviour. A pastor attached to the hospital is kept busy preaching and dealing with individual patients and their relatives, pointing them to Christ. Many have gone forth with restored physical health to start life anew with the companionship of the Son of God.

The Seton Maclures, like the Williams, were born into Christian homes and came to the knowledge of Christ as Saviour while still young. While reading theology at Christ's College, Cambridge, and at St. John's Hall, Highbury, Seton sensed the Lord's call to overseas service. He offered to the China Inland Mission, believing this to be the place to which the Lord was directing him. He was accepted, but advised to serve a curacy in England before sailing. So he accepted a title to Leyland Parish Church and was ordained in 1939.

Although this delay was a disappointment to him, he discovered that the Lord's hand was in it. The church was missionary-hearted and prayerful, and he learned much from his time there.

The vicar, the Rev. Peto, had two daughters, and during his curacy, Seton fell in love with Peggy, and they became engaged. She also felt called to China and had trained as a nurse. But when she applied, the door was closed on health grounds. As they sought the Lord's further guidance, however, the way opened to the West Nile District under the A.I.M.

Seton is a linguist, and it was not long before he mastered Lugbara. During the course of the years, he has gained a very thorough knowledge of the language. He led a committee consisting mostly of Africans in the translation of the Old Testament and the revision of the New Testament, his thorough grounding in Hebrew and Greek being of enormous help. This task took fifteen years. When at long last the first consignment of five thousand Lugbara Bibles arrived, they were sold out in less than a month.

At one period they occupied Goli station, a post among the Alur tribe, which had been opened in 1929. There he learned d'Alur. Later he turned his attention to Kakwa and other languages also. With the retirement of Archdeacon Vollor, Seton became the leader of the missionary work in the West Nile. Some years previously he and two of the African clergy had been made Canons of Namirembe Cathedral.

The Williams were not the only ones to have their parents on the field. On his retirement, Seton's father, Mr. H. S. Maclure, went to Arua and for a time helped with the book-keeping of the huge sums of money—from gifts, church offerings and government grants—which had to be accounted for in the Mission office at Arua; but the encroachments of chronic arthritis made it necessary for him to give up after about eighteen months.

When the missionaries evacuated from Congo, Dr. Becker and the staff from Oicha found an opportunity just over the border of Uganda at Nyabirongo, near Kasese. This developed into a large medical work. When the Congo staff returned, Dr. Keith Waddell, with African and European helpers, carried on the task which has continued to grow and shows much promise. Work has now been transferred to near-by Kagando.

This is, perhaps, the appropriate place to mention the East African Revival. This movement started in Ruanda in the early 1930s, when a number of Africans and Europeans came into blessing. It has since spread to the whole of East Africa and beyond, and thousands of nominal Christians have been brought into a vital experience of Christ.

In the pursuit of unhindered fellowship with the Lord, people are encouraged to confess individual sins before the group. The fact that the movement is independent of the organized churches, combined with some of its practices, has at times caused division. It has had its extreme section whose ways gave embarrassment. These eventually separated themselves from the main body, which is now working, for the most part, in closer co-operation with the churches.

PART SIX

CENTRAL AFRICAN REPUBLIC

Long Patience and Precious Fruit

25

Making a Start

UNCLE JOHN BUYSE was the one who safaried into what was then French Equatorial Africa prospecting for sites for mission stations. He left Kasengu in October 1923. There were no motor roads, and he had to travel on narrow native tracks. It was no easy task. The overhanging vegetation, wet with dew, soaked his clothing, and the sharp blades of the sword grass cut his knees and soon ruined his khaki shorts. On and on he travelled, day after day, from the hills of Kasengu, through the gentler savannah country to the north and west, into Azandeland, where the lower altitude and heavier vegetation together with the ironstone soil added to the heat of the journey. Every evening he gathered the people around him under the stars and told 'the old, old story of Jesus and His love'.

He took observations on all his journeys and prepared maps of the country. He started off by bicycle on which there was a milometer so that he could record the distance from one point to another. But before the end of the safari his bicycle gave out and he had to go on foot. Not to be beaten, however, he had an African push the front wheel, to which the milometer was attached, along the paths.

At long last, having left all trace of civilization behind him, and out of touch with the outside world, he crossed into French territory. He travelled round the area, and, after comparing various sites, he recommended that work be started at Zemio. He erected a small mud hut, and there he lived while awaiting the first missionaries who should settle there.

In January 1924 M. and Mme. Marc Forissier from France, and Mr. and Mrs. Boyson, Americans who had been studying French in Paris, set out from Bordeaux. They went by boat to Matadi on the West Coast and thence up the Congo River to Bangui, eventually reaching Zemio. There they met Uncle John. He spent some time with them, introducing them to missionary work.

The second party, consisting of Mr. Charles G. Hurlburt, a son of the General Director, with his wife, Mr. and Mrs. Ralph T. Davis and three single ladies, gathered at Bafuka, the most northerly of the Congo stations. They set out in two groups in July 1925. Sleeping sickness was rife on the shortest route, and the parties were only allowed to take the barest of necessities with them because porters were not permitted to cross the border. Ralph and Ellen Davis therefore took charge of the main baggage of the whole party, and followed a much longer route, via Bangassou. This involved the employment of nearly four hundred porters to take the goods to Bambili. This initial part of the journey occupied two weeks. From there to Bondo—about 200 miles—the baggage had to be taken by canoe on the Uele River.

But the local official at Bambili was bitterly anti-Protestant. Ralph had to approach him to ask permission to use the canoes. He refused. Ralph did his best to persuade him to change his mind, but all to no effect.

'If you cannot give permission, is there not a higher official we can approach?' asked Ralph.

'Only the Commissaire de District,' replied the Administrator.

'Where may he be found?'

'He is several hundred miles away and you could never

reach him.'

It seemed to Ralph and Ellen Davis that they had reached an impasse. There appeared to be no way out.

But there was a way up! They returned to the rest-house where they were staying. Then in prayer they told the Lord of their predicament, told Him of the official's attitude and asked Him to cause this man to change his mind.

During the short-lived tropical twilight, Ralph decided to step out for a little walk before the darkness set in completely. As he did so he descried a figure approaching in the dusk. He could not make out whether it was European or African. Should he address him in French or Bangala? He decided that it was better to err on the side of French, so he greeted him in that language. The decision was right. The Belgian was very affable, and before long Ralph was telling him of their trouble, how they were expecting to make the canoe trip but had been refused permission by the Administrator who had told him that only the Commissaire could give permission. Unfortunately he was very far away and it would be impossible to reach him.

Quietly the stranger said, 'I am the Commissaire. I will help you.'

Ralph gasped.

It was a miracle!

Canoes were promised for the river trip, and the Commissaire wrote letters to the Administrators at Bondo and Monga, asking them to help with porters.

The journey down the river was exciting. There were rapids which had to be 'shot' and others so dangerous that all that could be done was to unload the goods, carry them round the hazards and then reload them on the canoes. Notes such as the following occur in the diary which recounts the trip:

'September 14th. We passed one or two bad places, enjoyed a good breakfast of fried potatoes and chicken and coffee in the canoe. We passed one bad turn where the canoe with the motorbike hit a rock and nearly upset. Another time we passed over a spot where years ago in wartime a canoe full of Bankangos were fleeing and nearly a hundred were drowned due to overloading, and our canoemen all kept quiet when passing that spot.'

So they continued for nine days and were thankful when the trip came to an end. They had reached Bondo, where there was a station of the Norwegian Baptist Mission. There they had to wait for two months while the canoes returned to Bambili to bring the rest of the goods. They had had to leave them in a shed there as there were not sufficient canoes available to bring them all at one time. But the days were not wasted. Ralph had many opportunities of preaching at the services. His contacts with the Belgians at the Government Office were used to witness to the Gospel, and at the same time his French was improving.

In time he acquired a very good knowledge of the language. When he went to stay with his wife's relatives in Switzerland, her brothers took a delight in teaching him all the colloquialisms they could find. Consequently, when talking to officials, they could never disguise their 'asides' by using slang, as they could with the rest of us who knew only 'orthodox' French. He knew it all.

It was nearing the end of November before they were able to leave Bondo, with a large party of 376 porters carrying the goods. On 2nd December they crossed the frontier into French territory and arrived at Bangassou. They called on the official. He and his wife were coloured people who had been highly educated at the Sorbonne in

Above: An old-type African Church and its congregation.

Below: Church at Adi in Congo erected by African gifts and labour.

Overleaf: An A.I.M. Bible School student witnessing to a Turkana tribesman.

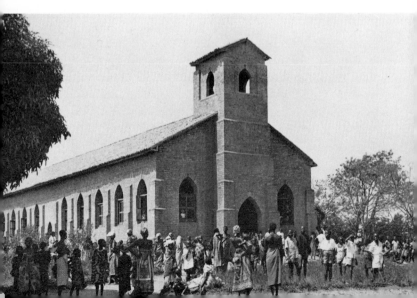

Paris. Missionaries of a Society which worked in Bangassou
had rendered great help to them, and they were therefore
very well disposed towards Protestant missionaries. They
supplied the Davises with food, and even lent them francs
to pay for rations for the porters, since they had exhausted
their ready cash and there was no means of cashing
cheques there.

Ralph was able to accompany Madame Eboué on her
grand piano while she sang. This pleased them greatly.
Most of the people who passed through could only play
jazz, and they appreciated the fact that Ralph played
classical music. He also played hymns and bore witness
to them. His fingers were stiff since he had had no opportunity to practise for a long time; but he did his best,
nevertheless.

Their favour having been won, the official and his wife
did all they could to help them. Monsieur Eboué supplied
all the porters they needed for the next stage of their
journey, and when Ralph ran into difficulties over the
payment of the men, he sent a soldier to settle the affair,
and to order them to take the goods all the way to Zemio
—a safari of two weeks duration.

'Moreover,' he said, 'they will not go for you, but for
the State. I will send soldiers along to look after them.
You and your wife will not need to travel with them, but
will leave a few days later.'

After the porters had left, he gave them his own 'tip-
pois' (carrying chairs), and porters to carry them both. And
all this was at the expense of the State!

Thus the Lord undertook for them. He saw that Ralph
was exhausted and so made this provision for him to be
carried. It was his first experience of this form of transport!

Ralph often referred to these days in his deputation
addresses. He would recall the fact that when he was

young he had to be *made* to practise the piano, but years later it was used of the Lord to gain the friendship and help of a French official in Central Africa.

Passing through Rafai, they eventually reached Zemio on 4th January 1925. The Charles Hurlburts were there. Bety Hurlburt and Ellen Davis were sisters and had much to talk about. There was much rejoicing and plenty of laughter. On the 25th they left for Djema, where they were to work. They erected a small grass hut in which to live. What a joy it was to be settled, even in such a shack after having been 171 days on the move since they left Bafuka! They had preached the Gospel all along the way, and though they were not given to see much in the way of results, certain it is that the Word given out did not return void.

Uncle John made another long safari in the territory, seeking places for other stations farther west. Eventually he reached Bangassou, where another Society was at work. The hardness of the path had reduced his clothing to rags and tatters. He dared not appear in the township in such a condition. So he made a detour and reached the mission station by another route.

It was Christmas Eve 1925 when this strange apparition presented himself. He looked as if he had come from a circus. His khaki shorts were in shreds. On one leg was a huge lavender and yellow patch. The other had been repaired with some red-striped material. Other rents had simply been sewn together. His shirt was in a similar condition, and its original material could scarcely be discovered.

The missionaries welcomed him. When he appeared for the evening meal, he was clad in pyjamas, which he laughingly described as his 'evening dress'; but they were all he had. He found no place where he could replace his worn-out garments. He had reminded the Lord of his need. God could furnish a table in the wilderness; but could He furnish clothes?

Christmas morning came. A substitute Christmas tree stood in a corner of the living-room. Below it were arranged parcels of all sorts and sizes. Among them to his great surprise were two for John Buyse! When the time came to open them, he found that each contained a pair of khaki shorts, a shirt and other small items. It overwhelmed him. Tears of joy rolled down the cheeks of the erstwhile tough sailor. The Lord had met his need! The lady of the house had noted his condition when he arrived. She had some khaki drill on hand with which she had intended to make shorts for her husband; but in view of Uncle John's need, she sat up late that night and made them up for him. A while before, a friend had sent a parcel of shirts to give away as she saw the need. She enclosed one of them in each of the parcels and added a few handkerchiefs and other things. So the Lord provided.

John remained in French Equatorial Africa long enough to get the work started, and then made the long safari back to Kasengu.

26

A Time to Sow

ALTHOUGH so much of miracle had marked the opening of the work in French Equatorial Africa, there were many ups and downs during the first few years. The party which entered were soon settled on three stations. John Buyse wrote at this time:

'We have three stations which form a triangle. Obo to the east, Zemio to the west and Djema to the north. They are situated on low ridges, affording a good outlook over the surrounding territory and sufficiently distanced from streams to prevent possible visits and infection from the tsetse fly. (The tsetse fly is the carrier of sleeping sickness.) Each is supplied with excellent drinking water bubbling forth from the inner recesses of the station hill. There is also a goodly quantity of big and small timber for building purposes and burning bricks. ...'

One of the single ladies who went in with the party from Bafuka was Gertrude Weber from Switzerland. She served in French Equatorial Africa for thirty-five years, and died in harness. During that period she only took four furloughs. She saw many changes in personnel. There were eleven on the field in 1925. Eight years later, she was the only one left of them. Charles Hurlburt had passed away. Madame Forissier's health was very poor, as was also that of their baby, and they had to go home in June 1926. Others left for various reasons. There were times during the ensuing years when Gertrude Weber was alone in the work. Sometimes she had two or three fellow-workers. Latterly the number increased to twelve. However, few or many, she carried on faithfully. The Hubers, who worked with her for some years, wrote:

'Miss Weber faithfully worked and prayed with us, cooperating in a wonderful way. A deeply spiritual woman, she never counted the cost in any service rendered to the Lord.'

By 1926 the Davises had spent more than six years in Africa, and their health was not good. Ellen suggested to her husband that they should pray for provision to be made for them to go on furlough, as if they did not, she feared that she would have to bury him there. But Ralph was reluctant, and said:

'The only way I would be willing to leave would be under two conditions: First, if the money comes into our hands without our making mention of the need to anyone. And second, if a baby should be expected.'

The nearest doctor was 800 miles away.

Within a very short time, both these conditions were met, and they 'gathered assuredly' that the Lord would have them go. Accordingly, some three months later, in November, they left for Switzerland. Mr. and Mrs. Alber came from Obo and took their places at Djema.

Gradually the staff diminished until only Miss Weber and Mr. and Mrs. Boyson were left. Miss Weber went on furlough in 1930 and did not return until 1932.

By the time she returned, Mr. and Mrs. Lester Huber

had arrived. They were already serving in Congo, but at a Field Conference in 1931 they volunteered to go to the French field in view of the great need for workers there. The Boysons left shortly afterwards, and for a time the Hubers and Gertrude Weber comprised the whole of the missionary staff.

Little had been done in the way of building and all the houses were of mud. The thatched roofs leaked badly. Not only was there a shortage of workers, funds were very low too. The three did all they could, going out to the villages and preaching the Gospel, conducting classes for reading and writing on the station and carrying on simple medical work. There were many difficulties, and every possible obstacle was thrown in their way by the local French official, whose wife was a bigoted Roman Catholic.

Lester Huber made a long tour of the countryside by bicycle, staying away for two months, preaching the evangel in places where it had never been heard before. The Holy Spirit worked through these and other meetings which were held, and people who 'had turned from idols to serve the living and true God' brought their fetishes to the mission station and gave stirring testimonies of their faith in Christ.

It came as a severe shock when the local Administrator told Mr. Huber that he must erect permanent buildings without delay on the site which had been granted at Zemio. What could they do? They had no money for buildings. They had no brick machine with which to make bricks. There was no cement to be had and they would have to import it from Congo at great expense and pay heavy customs duty on top of that. And Mr. Huber had had no experience of building.

They did what has always been done when difficulties arise—they prayed. God laid the verses of Exodus 31 : 2–5 on Lester Huber's mind :

'See, I have called by name Bezaleel the son of Uri, the son of Hur, of the tribe of Judah; and I have filled him with the spirit of God, in wisdom, and in understanding, and in all manner of workmanship, to devise cunning works, to work in gold, and in silver, and in brass, and in cutting of stones, to set them, and in carving of timber, to work in all manner of workmanship.'

In due course, with the Lord's undertaking, two substantial brick houses were erected, and are still in use today.

To missionaries, especially those in difficult places, the Lord is very real. He is their recourse in the face of all opposition and obstacles. But perhaps it is at times of personal crisis that the Lord's presence is realized most clearly.

An experience of the Hubers is typical of those of very many of the Lord's servants. While at Zemio, three children were born to them. The second, a boy, was taken from them at the age of fifteen months. Mr. Huber had to conduct the funeral himself. He had to preach in French for the benefit of the doctor and local merchants who attended and in Pazande for the Africans. The Lord transformed this into a peak experience in their lives. Their hearts were filled with abounding joy as they realized that their babe was in the presence of Christ for ever, and that they would yet see him again. Their conduct made a deep impression on the Africans who said:

'Now we see that the things that the Bwana and Madame have taught us are real.'

They were also very impressed by the fact that the parents went back fearlessly into the house where the child had died. The heathen would never do such a thing; they would destroy the house in which a death had occurred.

Shortly before the Hubers left for their first furlough in 1938, their supply of milk failed. They were reduced to one cup of goat's milk a day, and Mrs. Huber was giving that to a baby whose mother was suffering from septicaemia. Mr. Van Dusen from Congo had planned to make a trip to Zemio and had promised to bring a supply of powdered milk. But just at that time there were rumours of an outbreak of Yellow Fever in French Equatorial Africa. The Belgian officials, hearing of this, told him that he could leave Congo if he wanted to, but they would not allow him back if he did so. So he could not bring the promised supplies. The local merchant had no tinned milk, and was leaving for Bangui, 800 miles away, to replenish his stocks; but they could not wait for his return. Their need was urgent, for they had two children who were dependent on milk. Mrs. Huber went to their little office, knelt down and cried to the Lord regarding their need. She laid hold upon the promises, reminding the Lord that through all the difficult days of the past He had never failed them. Turning to the Scriptures for a reassuring word, her eyes fell upon Proverbs 27 : 27 :

'And thou shalt have goat's milk for thy food, for the food of thy household, and for the maintenance of thy maidens.'

She went to her husband and said joyfully :

'God is going to give us goat's milk.'

He read the verse. But where could goat's milk be found? As far as they knew, theirs were the only goats for miles and miles; and they were dry.

The next day Miss Weber went to the government post as she did each Thursday to give a flannelgraph talk. This she did in the open air. As she was giving it, the merchant came along and interrupted her. He said that he was leaving for his long journey on the morrow and added:

'I have plenty of goats' milk that the Mission can have if you send someone for it every day. Months ago I went up into the Lake Chad area and purchased a flock of goats of a good strain.'

Thus God knew of the need long before it occurred and sent this man on a 3,000-mile trip in order to supply it. There was an abundance of fresh milk which lasted until the Hubers left for furlough some months later.

27

Faithful Toil

IN 1939 Gertrude Weber was joined by the John Linquists. They were destined to play a leading part in the work of that field. Both Marguerite and John had been converted in early years, and had long had their eyes on the mission field. Accepted by the Mission, they were soon initiated into the testings of the Faith life, and of the Lord's faithful provision in the nick of time. They were to go to France to study French before proceeding to Africa. The day before they left, they still lacked a hundred and twenty dollars to cover their expenses. But the Lord was not unmindful of them. Before the train left next morning, ten separate gifts came, in answer to prayer alone, and they totalled one hundred and twenty dollars and seventy-five cents!

They spent six months in France, during which time John passed important examinations in the French language.

Because of the outbreak of the Second World War, the Hubers were detained in America until 1945. But before the Linquists went on their first furlough, the staff had been augmented by the coming of Mr. and Mrs. Lincoln and Miss Blanche Westgate.

The work in this field has never been spectacular. The territory itself is difficult. The ironstone soil is very poor and unproductive. The Africans are naturally unstable and many of those who professed faith in Christ succumbed to the temptations to immorality which the tribal practices made so easy. The missionaries have plodded on faithfully, sowing the seed and watering it with their prayers. One of them recorded:

'Day after day two or three hours were spent in intercessory prayer for this work and the work of the Mission as a whole.'

But results came slowly, and all too often when the missionaries were encouraged by responses, their bright hopes were cast down before long. Yet there were those who stood.

At a special service one Easter Sunday at Rafai, the Gospel was preached to a large gathering. At its conclusion twenty-three professed conversion. Although the missionaries did not know it, one was a chief who lived 100 miles up river. A year passed, and they heard nothing of him. Then he came to visit them and asked if he might be allowed to come with his wife and children and live on the station so that he could learn to read. Permission was gladly given. While he was there his behaviour gave ample testimony to his having been born again, and the Hubers could see that he was a devoted Christian. He was eager to tell others of his Saviour and to bring them into like saving faith with himself.

He was a man of some importance, having been awarded a number of French decorations. Yet he said:

'Being chief is not a big thing in my eyes. I'm the Lord's servant. I've built a chapel in my village and I want all my people to believe in Jesus.'

He himself took an active part in teaching the things of God and maintained a bright testimony.

Others there were and are. They have been the outstanding leaders. But there are also men and women, not in such prominent positions, who maintained a testimony which shone all the brighter against the dark background of heathen custom. Their courageous witness demonstrated the power of Christ made perfect on the platform of human weakness.

Slowly the number of missionaries built up. It was a severe blow when, in 1957, Cleo Mann, a most promising missionary, was taken ill with cerebral malaria and passed away suddenly. The political disturbances in Congo meant that some of the personnel from there were released for service in what is now the Central African Republic. The troubles in Southern Sudan have resulted in large numbers of refugees streaming into the Republic. These have settled in camps and present a large opportunity for Gospel ministry, and some of the missionaries and African evangelists are taking advantage of it.

When it was a French Colony, medical work by the Missions was not encouraged; but since the territory has become independent, doors are wide open for this avenue of service. The dispensary at Rafai is well attended and growing. Others have now been opened at Obo and Zemio. There is a need for a doctor, especially as the section is inadequately served medically.

PART SEVEN

SOUTHERN SUDAN
Scattered Blossoms

28

Sowing and Sorrow

JOHN BUYSE'S eyes had built-in telescopes. They were ever looking beyond. Wherever the people were still in darkness and the Gospel not being preached, he longed to go. He pioneered in Congo, in the West Nile District and in French Equatorial Africa; but he was not satisfied. He turned his attention to the unoccupied areas of Southern Sudan. From time to time he gathered his things together and made safaris into those parts, and pressed the Mission authorities to open work there.

It was not possible to respond immediately. Only in 1949 was the new advance made. There was no question as to who should lead it. It could be no other than John and Mabel Buyse. In company with Rev. and Mrs. Beatty they went to Opari, where there was an outpost which had been started by the Church Missionary Society. But they had not been able to supervise the area, and were glad to hand it over to the A.I.M.

There was one residence there. It had curious curved walls back and front, and 'Aunt Mabel' with her ready wit promptly dubbed it 'The Egg'. It consisted of three small rooms, and for a time it had to house four adults and a baby!

Shortly after, two single ladies arrived, and a 'Medical Department' was opened under a spreading tree, and a

Girls' School was commenced. Before long, temporary buildings were erected and a start made on learning Arabic—the official language. The Acholi tongue which is the vernacular of that part is akin to the Alur language which John and Mabel knew well; so they were able to understand and be understood. In the townships there were always some who knew Bangala, the lingua franca of north-east Congo.

Water was the big problem, however. The shortage was severe. The Sudanese Government insisted that no permanent buildings be erected until a good water supply was assured. They had planned to open a station at Katire Ayom and make it the headquarters; but the granting of the site was made contingent on the finding of sufficient water. Nor could Opari concession be granted until the building programme at Katire Ayom was completed.

Everything hinged on the question of water. They commenced digging a well, shovelful by shovelful over a period of six months; but they struck no water. Then the rains came and put a stop to digging.

It seemed hopeless. They spread the matter before the Lord and anxiously awaited the next word from the Government. Someone suggested that what they needed was a drilling rig; but that seemed out of the question. Even if money were provided for such an expensive piece of equipment, who would operate it? It was a job for a specialist. In any case, government geophysicists were rumoured to have surveyed the whole region and had said that no water was to be found.

Yet the Lord did the seeming impossible. A friend of the Lord's work in America presented a drilling rig. It was a long, long time on the way, but at length it arrived. The Congo field loaned Earl Dix—the handiest of all handymen to run it.

Earl Dix is one who specializes in the impossible. Talk

Left:
Giving the 'go ahead' signal in A.I.M.'s radio studio.

Below:
A Christian Book Centre in Kenya.

Right: Missionary nursing sister tucks a newborn in for the night while the mother looks on proudly.

Below: An operation in progress in an A.I.M. hospital.

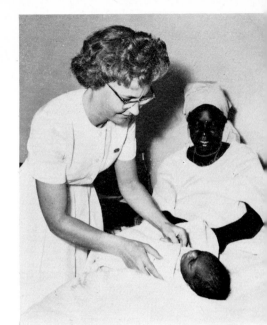

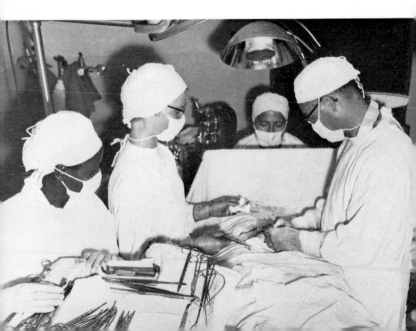

of an impossible job, or one that is too difficult, and he will butt in with his 'Wait a minute' and he is ready to show that it can be done and he will do it. And he does! He always brings a poem to mind, part of which says:

> 'Somebody said that it couldn't be done
> But he with a chuckle replied,
> That maybe it couldn't, but he would be one
> Who wouldn't say so till he'd tried.
> So he butted right in with the trace of a grin
> On his face; if he worried he hid it.
> He started to sing as he tackled the thing
> That couldn't be done, and he did it.'

Within a couple of months of the arrival of the machine he had drilled four wells in the Sudan field—at Katire Ayom, Opari, Torit and Logotok—all successful. The one at Logotok was 200 feet deep. The Government was amazed, and their geophysicists had to change their ideas. Mr. Dix was able to drill a couple of wells for the Government and the amount they paid for these covered the heavy customs and transport on the machine.

Miracle again! Such experiences 'above all that we ask or think' are exhilarating, but humbling. How little our faith in such a wonder-working God!

The work in Southern Sudan was helped from its earliest days by African missionaries, sent out and partly supported by their home churches in Congo. They had received training in one or other of the Bible Schools in Congo before going to Sudan. They did faithful service for many years until the situation became untenable and they had to leave.

Simeona Nzia and his wife Phoebe went from Adza. As an ordained man Simeona was greatly used in the township of Torit and the surrounding area.

Metusila Uzele went from Rethy and, with his wife Ana, worked among the most backward people of the Latuka tribe at Logotok. These people are steeped in heathenism, and have a contempt for clothing. Yet from among them trophies of grace have come, and a little nucleus of believers exists. Metusila had been a member of the team which accompanied Austin Paul and assisted him in his evangelistic campaigns. Besides taking his turn at preaching, Metusila played the cornet and trombone. When conditions became disturbed in Sudan, he went to Kenya and enrolled at the Scott Theological College. When he had completed the course there, he was asked to lead the evangelistic work in Kenya in the 'Evangelism for All' campaigns.

Andarea Vumi went from Sudan to Congo for Bible training and worked among his own people—the Madi. Others followed his example, including his two sons.

In spite of the many obstacles which had to be overcome, the Lord worked, even among the darkest and most ignorant. Maria Magadala had lived a life of debauchery, drinking and immorality. She left all to follow Christ after hearing the good news of salvation. She gave the following public testimony on one occasion:

'If you people here knew how great a Saviour I have, you would want Him too. I was the vilest of sinners. I slept with my pipe and had to have beer every day and all that goes with that sort of life. I had hunger for those things as man has hunger for a drink of water. But now I am free, for He, the Lord Jesus, has come into my life and old things have passed away.'

Maria was most ardent in her zeal. She attended every meeting and was always on hand to give ready help in the practical and mundane tasks which have to be done.

She missed no opportunity of telling others of her Saviour.

Hopes rose high when a doctor and his wife offered for the work in Sudan. Dr. and Mrs. Reitsma went to the field in 1951 to open a hospital at Logotok. They had to commence from scratch. The best they could do was to erect mud huts. These served as wards for the housing of a few in-patients, and one of them was used as a clinic. In these primitive conditions, the doctor performed operations, electric light being provided by portable generators.

But the work at Logotok was not allowed to develop. It suffered one setback after another. In 1954 tribal warfare broke out, culminating in the burning of the hospital and the doctor's house.

To the surprise of everyone, Rev. and Mrs. Sidney Langford, who had served many years in Congo and were doing an excellent work at Aba, asked to be transferred to the Sudan. They went at first to Logotok, but when John and Mabel Buyse went on furlough in 1952, the Langfords moved to Torit and Sidney Langford became Field Director. He was faced with many problems. Political conditions were troubled. The powerful Northerners, who were Moslems, sought to subdue the Southern tribes, who were mostly pagan.

Independence came to Sudan on 1st January 1955. Before long, however, the new Government was in trouble with many of the tribes people, which culminated in a mutiny among the Southern Sudan Defence Force. Reinforcements from the north soon quelled the opposition; but the trouble was driven underground. A military coup which took place in Khartoum in 1958 changed the political colour, but made no difference in the general attitude of the Southerners. The whole of the southern and eastern provinces have been under a state of emergency since then.

In 1955 Sidney Langford was appointed General Secretary of the Mission in America. His place as Field Director was taken by Rev. Harold Amstutz who, with his wife, had worked at Adza in Congo and built up a prosperous indigenous church.

Conditions remained unsettled, and the work was constantly under restriction of one kind or another imposed by the Government. In 1956 all educational work was taken over by the State, apart from very simple classes to teach the people to read. Two years later, these also were stopped. Village and market meetings were banned. Missionaries were not allowed to travel without permission. These restrictions were followed by a heavier blow when all medical work was taken over by the Government, and the Reitsmas were ordered to leave the country.

Missionaries who went on furlough found it difficult to obtain visas to return. To some they were denied, as they were to all new missionaries.

As late as 1957 new work had been commenced. It was among the Taposa people at a place called Riwoto. The Bible Churchmen's Missionary Society had opened work there earlier, but it had not prospered. There was no church and only a handful of adherents. The people as a whole were pagans, although the Catholics had a following.

But conditions deteriorated and more and more restrictions were imposed. The 'Missionary Societies Act' rigorously curtailed their activities. The Southerners carried on guerrilla warfare against the Northerners, and this provoked reprisals. Conditions became so serious that in 1963 the missionaries at Opari and Katire Ayom were told to move to another station since the Government could not give them protection. The order was also given that all travel must be done in military convoy.

In November of that year, Harold and Jane Amstutz were travelling in convoy from Torit to Juba when they came under fire from a band of guerrillas, who mistook their Land-Rover for a military vehicle, and Harold was wounded. He was taken to the hospital at Juba and treated there.

Events moved quickly and in February 1964 all of the two hundred and sixty Roman Catholic missionaries and the forty Protestant in the three southern provinces were ordered to leave. The Sudan Government sought to blame the continuing unrest on the presence of missionaries; but as far as the Protestant missionaries were concerned, at any rate, the charge was without foundation. Harold and Jane Amstutz were the last to leave. He had endeavoured by every possible means to negotiate a change in the government edict; but without success. The only gesture of encouragement given was that the Government had 'no charge' against the A.I.M. but, 'on the contrary, they are held in high regard'.

Refugees poured across the borders into Uganda, Congo and the Central African Republic. The pastors and evangelists continued to care for their little flocks as long as they could; but the time came when most of them came to the conclusion that they too must flee. Hiding in the bush, sleeping in the open, they stealthily made their ways, with their families, until they found themselves in the safety of neighbouring countries.

The expelled missionaries found work in the other fields of the Mission. Just at that time the General Field Secretary became seriously ill and was invalided home. Harold Amstutz, released from responsibilities in the Sudan, was available at precisely the right time to take the position.

One of the evangelists who remained on as long as he dared was one of the first Latuka Christians. When he came to work at Logotok in 1951 he was quite illiterate and still pagan. He asked if he might attend school and learn to read. Permission was readily given and he proved to be an apt pupil. Martha Hughell employed him to help in the house. In the school he heard the Gospel message daily, and also attended devotions in the home. He came into living faith in Christ in 1953 and there was a very apparent change in his life and attitude. He seemed to grasp spiritual truth and to love the Lord. Two years later he was baptized and took the name of Tomasi. His love for the Word and concern for those around him led him to go to the Bible School at Adi in the Congo. His studies there and his contact with older Christians deepened his spiritual life and gave him larger vision and understanding.

He was not married at that time. When he read in the Word of God that Christians should not be unequally yoked with unbelievers (2 Cor. 6 : 14) he was very concerned. He sought out one of the missionary teachers and asked what he should do, for there were no Christian girls among the Latuka. He was advised to make it a matter of prayer, and together they brought the problem before the Lord. Tomasi returned to his tribe in the expectancy that in some way or other the Lord would undertake. The waiting time was hard. Once the temptation overcame him and he fell into sin. He was deeply repentant, and as a result of the experience was more cast upon his Saviour. At last, however, his faith was rewarded and a suitable girl was converted, and he felt free to marry her.

Tomasi carried on the work at Logotok after the missionaries had left. There were only eleven church members there, and he was the only one with any stability. Before two years had elapsed, however, the situation became such that he found it wise to make his escape. Travelling by night and hiding in the bush by day, he and his wife and children gradually made their way until they had crossed the border into Uganda. Once in the safety of that country they were able to breathe freely again. Since they all needed medical attention, they went to the Mission hospital at Kuluva. There they were given physical and material help.

But as soon as they were fit, Tomasi left, and went north to the border where thousands of Sudan refugees were gathered in huge camps. There he, with others, preached the Gospel to those who because of their extremity were prepared in heart to listen.

PART EIGHT
COMMON GROUND

29

Mission Organization

THE year 1955 was an important one in the history of the Africa Inland Mission. The fact that it was the sixtieth anniversary of its founding was incidental. The main event was the inauguration of a revised constitution in a series of special meetings at Kijabe in Kenya.

The new constitution had been under discussion for a number of years. It brought the whole Mission in its various parts into a closer unity. On the field a General Field Secretary was provided for, and a Central Field Council on which all the fields were represented.

An International Conference was envisaged, consisting of representatives from each of the Home Councils and the Central Field Council. The post of International General Secretary was created, although the title was afterwards changed to that of General Director.

The International Conference was made responsible for general Mission policy and practice, while the Central Field Council was to be the co-ordinating authority for the work of the Mission throughout the field.

The conservative doctrinal foundation of the Mission and its faith basis were reaffirmed.

Ralph T. Davis, who had been General Secretary in America for many years, was elected the first International General Secretary, and Kenneth L. Downing, son of Lee H. Downing, became the first General Field Secretary. Ralph and Ellen Davis have already come to our notice in the early days of work in what is now the Central African Republic.

Ralph Tully Davis was born in 1895, the same year as the Mission, in East Orange, New Jersey. After graduating from high school, he began to learn the jewellery trade, but in 1915, while singing in the choir at some special meetings, he was moved to give his life to the Lord for whole-time service. The idea of working overseas had not entered his head then, and he considered taking up work with the Y.M.C.A.

His godly mother realized that if he were to win souls, the first essential was a knowledge of the Word of God. She therefore advised him to go to a good Bible School. Accordingly the autumn of 1917 found him at the Moody Bible Institute, Chicago.

While he was there, Bwana Hurlburt addressed the students, after which a special day of prayer for Africa was held. It was then that Ralph heard the call to that continent.

Only a few months after commencing his studies at the Bible Institute he was called up for military service. He had been turned down previously as a heart murmur was discovered; but he was passed this time, and on 5th March 1918 he became a soldier in the Medical Corps. He served for eighteen months, nine of which were spent in France.

During the time he had been at the Moody Bible Institute he had met Ellen Ortlieb, a young lady of Swiss extraction who was already an accepted candidate for service in Africa. Her sister was already on the field, being the wife of Charles G. Hurlburt. She passed away in childbirth, and some years later, Charles went to Switzerland, and married the youngest of the three sisters, Bety.

Ralph and Ellen became engaged before he joined the army, and soon after his discharge, they were married.

Not long after this, Ralph passed through an experience which deepened and enriched his life. They were members of the Moody Memorial Church. The Rev. Paul Rader was its pastor at that time, and he exercised a profound influence on the lives of both Ralph and Ellen. One Sunday he spoke on Missionary Work and made an appeal for young men to come forward. Ellen Davis tells the story in the following words:

'Suddenly, without a word, Ralph left my side and went forward. I wondered why, as I knew that he was completely surrendered to go to Africa. When he returned he told me that the Lord had spoken to him to be willing to go *anywhere* and not to specify Africa because he knew he wanted to be in a warm climate as he disliked the cold. He said, "I told the Lord that I'd be willing to go to *Alaska* if that was the place He wanted me to go, and that I would have no strings upon my life, *anywhere* would be alright with me." It was only a few days after that when the way opened for us to leave for Africa, passages and support all promised.'

'No strings on my life. Anywhere would be alright with me'—there undoubtedly lay the secret of his great influence and usefulness. He had no reserves. He held nothing back.

They went forth in 1920 as missionaries of the Moody Memorial Church. At first they went to Rhodesia, but after a short while they transferred to Congo. They met Mr. Hurlburt at Kijabe in East Africa and travelled the rest of the way by motor-cycle and sidecar. The Lake Albert steamer took them from Butiaba to Panyamur. From there the escarpment rises steeply. It was too much for the motor-cycle, and it had to be pushed. This was very exhausting. They paid Africans to help, but before long they ran out of ready cash with which to pay them. All they could do was to give promissory notes, and to send a man back later to redeem them.

Crossing over into Congo, the Davises were appointed to open a station among the Kakwa, while awaiting developments regarding the new work in French Equatorial Africa. The site originally applied for had been refused by the Government. Application was made for another, but there was a long delay in granting it, owing to the unfriendly attitude of the local Administrator. Before the permit came through, the way began to open into the French territory.

When my wife and I reached the Congo in 1924, we were asked to take over the Kakwa work. At the end of four days' hot and tiring safari from Aba, we arrived there. The Davises made us welcome, and since they knew Bangala by that time, he dealt with the porters who had carried our kit. A lifelong friendship developed between us.

Ralph's irrepressible humour was soon apparent, and we felt at home with them immediately. We have often recalled a day when, after we had unpacked, I was attempting to turn our packing cases into furniture. I had noticed in their house a table which could be folded for safari. I asked if I might see it, since I wanted to make a folding table.

'Man!' said he. 'My trouble is to make one that won't fold!'

After a few weeks, during which they initiated us into African ways, they left. They were to make their way to Bafuka, to join the party waiting to enter French Equatorial Africa. They travelled as far as Aba with Mr. and Mrs. Jim Bell. There were then no motor roads in those parts, and all travel had to be on native paths. They set out on a motor-cycle and sidecar along the main path from Aru to Aba. It was the time of the heavy rains. There are numerous streams along the way which ordinarily are mere trickles, but, after a downpour, they become raging torrents. The bridges over them were crude, consisting merely of poles. When they had covered about half the distance, they came to a stream which was in flood. The bridge, which was normally high above the water, was partly submerged. Its poles were loose and some had been swept away. But get across they must, by hook or by crook, and get the motor-cycle across too. They walked across several times to test its strength. It seemed reasonably safe, so Ellen Davis crossed to the farther bank. Then, with several Africans helping, the two men started to manipulate the machine across the doubtful bridge. But it was too much for the weakened structure. They were halfway across when the whole thing collapsed, and men and motor-cycle fell into the stream. The machine sank like lead and was lost to sight. The men found themselves in deep water. Jim Bell averred that he lost consciousness before being helped out. Ralph went up to his chin in the stream, but managed to find a footing and got out and was able to help Jim. Ellen had watched the calamity with much anxiety and was greatly relieved when the men were safe on the bank. They all regarded their deliverance as a miracle. There was a mud-and-wattle resthouse near by, and living on native potatoes and sleeping on heaps of grass, they managed to survive the two or three days until help arrived. Fortunately they had a mosquito net with them so that they were able to protect themselves from the swarming pests. When the waters had abated somewhat, they were able to retrieve the motor-cycle; but a lot of work was needed before it could be restored to running order.

In spite of its seriousness, those who knew Jim Bell and Ralph Davis can imagine the humour with which it was recounted; the former with his southern American accent, his long forefinger wagging as, with amusing exaggerations, he gave his version; Ralph with his quick repartee.

Ralph always had a quick and witty word for the occasion. Some years later, when he was stationed at Aba in the Congo, he had occasion to consult the Administrator. Forgetting that the day was a public holiday, he went to the office in the morning and was surprised to find it closed. He discovered, however, that although the doors were shut, the Official was at his desk inside. Ralph found his way in.

'Don't you know that it is the King's birthday?' queried the Administrator sharply.

'Yes,' retorted Ralph, 'but I thought he was born in the afternoon!'

The story of their long safari from Bafuka into French territory has already been told. When they returned after furlough, in 1928, they were assigned to Aba station in the Congo. Ralph was Station Superintendent and Legal Representative of the whole field to the Government. He was kept very busy, taking a daily service for the workmen, and preaching regularly at the church services. When they felt the need of a change, they would come to us at Adi for the weekend. There were motor roads by this time, and he had a car. Whenever we went to Aba, we stayed with them.

They went on their second furlough in 1935. He was an excellent speaker, and was asked to extend their furlough to engage in deputation ministry. He had the ability to 'tune in' to any audience. He travelled all over the United States and was greatly used. His emphasis was always on the spiritual.

Even so, his irrepressible humour often came out. His

love for coffee was a by-word. He was once visiting a Swedish church in Minnesota. There was a strong aroma of coffee as the ladies prepared the refreshments which were to follow the meeting. When Ralph stood up to speak he said:

'My name is Ralph *T*. Davis. The *T* stands for coffee.'

He was appointed Assistant General Secretary to the Rev. H. D. Campbell, who had been General Secretary in America since 1924. Mr. Campbell had seen missionary service in Western Congo where he had been a contemporary of Peter Cameron Scott. In 1941 Mr. Campbell was made General Secretary Emeritus and Ralph took his place as General Secretary.

His labours were prodigious; but he enjoyed his work. Rarely could he be persuaded to take a holiday, saying:

'I live in a vacation.'

Often he had to rise very early and could only retire to rest in the early hours of the next morning. He travelled long distances to speak at different churches. In between times of travelling and speaking he carried on his office responsibilities, dictating his letters wherever he was and posting the records back to the office for typing. The Lord had prepared him for this kind of work by giving him the ability to eat any kind of food and sleep on any kind of bed.

His appointment as International General Secretary relieved him of much of his responsibility in the office. His position as Secretary was taken by Sidney Langford of the Sudan field. But Ralph transferred his energies to other tasks. He was never still. His diary was always full. He had to be busy for his Lord. The only dates he could keep for his home and family were those he noted in his diary so that he could remember them.

When two invitations came to him for the same day, he would almost invariably accept that from the smaller church in preference to the larger one and to what seemed to be the greater opportunity, feeling that the smaller groups were more needy and at the same time more responsive.

His interests spilled out beyond the A.I.M. to the whole world. Five times he was chosen as President of the Interdenominational Foreign Missions Association of America, and served in that capacity for nine years. His advice, as a missionary statesman, was widely sought for and greatly valued.

In 1949 Wheaton College conferred on him the honorary degree of Doctor of Divinity.

But this strenuous life took its toll. In 1962 his health indicated that the time had come to retire. He had always held that nobody should hold an important office after the age of sixty-five; but the whole Mission had insisted on his carrying on longer. He and his wife decided to retire at Media, the home for retired A.I.M. missionaries in Florida. Many prophesied that the quiet life there would not suit him, and he would be restless and unhappy. But they were proved false. Once there he enjoyed the unhurried time for Bible study and prayer. He preached as occasion offered, and taught a Bible Class. Visitors came to see him and to ask his advice on their problems. Seldom did he let anyone leave without having prayer with them.

He carried on a large correspondence concerning mission matters, and edited a monthly leaflet *Fuel for Prayer Fires*, giving matters to be prayed for each day of the month.

The time of evening calm was not prolonged, however. He was called into the Lord's presence on 19th August 1963 following a heart attack. The evening before he had spoken to a group of young people concerning Christ's claim on their lives.

Following his homegoing, the American Council passed a resolution expressing their sorrow, and adding:

'We are mindful of his forty-two years of dedicated service and untiring efforts in the ministry of the Africa Inland Mission both out in Africa and in the homeland. Under God the work of the Mission has greatly prospered under his leadership. We who have laboured so close to him for many years thank God upon every remembrance of him and mourn the loss of his warmhearted fellowship and wise counsel.'

All the Councils of the Mission recorded similar expressions.

Since his departure, the office of General Director has remained vacant.

Kenneth Downing, after filling a number of important positions in the Kenya field, became the first General Field Secretary with great profit to the Mission, bringing the fields to a better understanding of one another. His wide experience and counsel were placed at the disposal of the Councils of the various fields. He and his wife Ivy became known and loved throughout the whole Mission. In 1961 they went on furlough, expecting to return to the same office. In the meantime, however, there was a request from a joint committee of the International Foreign Missions Association and the Evangelical Foreign Missions Association for the release of Ken Downing to open a centre in Nairobi for the encouragement of the formation of Evangelical Fellowships throughout Africa. At first he was very reluctant to undertake this task; but the field recognized the need for it and persuaded him to agree. The step has been greatly blessed of God, and nobody can doubt that it was brought about by the Holy Spirit.

His place during furlough and until early 1964 was taken by the writer. When I had to lay it down, Harold Amstutz from Sudan was available to step into the position. God had His man ready at the right time. His experience in Congo and Sudan had prepared Harold Amstutz for the post.

The first Home Council of the work was in America, but after Bwana Hurlburt's visit to England in 1904 a small committee was set up there, and it was enlarged when he went there again in 1911, and it would appear that it was then recognized as a Council. In the early days the Mission was very little known in England, and the American branch undertook to help with the support of British missionaries. By 1928, however, it was felt that the British end should be self-supporting, and funds were no longer sent from the United States. This cast the British Council on the Lord in a new way. At first there was a time of severe testing, but the Lord honoured the faith, and for many years full allowances were paid to British missionaries.

The rule made under the new Constitution was that, in order to be recognized as a Council by the International Conference, a country must have at least ten missionaries on the field fully supported for not less than three years. Canada had already qualified when the new Constitution was put into effect; so a Canadian Council was recognized in 1955, Australia following in 1962. Others are expected to qualify before long.

The missionary force now includes members from America, Canada, Great Britain, Eire, Germany, Switzerland, Austria, South Africa, Australia and New Zealand.

30

Church Organization

DURING the 1930s, the attention of missionaries in Kenya, Tanzania and Congo was directed towards the organization of the churches which had been brought into being. The time had come for national Christians to take over the main responsibility for church affairs. Accordingly, committees were set up in each of the three main fields to consider the matter.

For denominational missions, such occasions do not arise; the pattern of church government is already set. But with interdenominational missions with their varied backgrounds, drawing up a scheme of church organization is not easy. It was decided in the main not to follow any existing church pattern, but to study the Scriptures afresh to seek to discover the Lord's will.

In Kenya and Congo similar plans were adopted. While leaning to the Baptist, or Congregational type of government, it bore some resemblance to Presbyterianism. The original schemes, while giving the commanding majority to Africans, had a place for missionaries on their various councils. This worked very well. As time went on, the plans were modified to bring them abreast of the times. After some twenty years it was felt in Congo that the constitution needed revising. A committee of church leaders and missionaries was appointed to do this task.

The new scheme gave the whole of the government of the church into the hands of Congolese. Under the guidance of God, the constitution was produced precisely at the right time. Stimulated by political propaganda, there was on every hand a forceful urge towards independence. This had not yet become vocal in church circles; but when the revised constitution was promulgated, it was welcomed with acclamation. It came into effect a few months before Independence was granted to Congo, and when, later in the year, most of the missionaries had to leave, the church was already prepared to carry on. And so it has done since, and the blessing of God has rested upon it.

The scheme provided for a local council, composed of elected members from each church in an area—usually, but not necessarily, that covered by one mission station. The whole field was divided into districts, and the local councils appointed their delegates to a District Church Council. The District Councils, in their turn, elected their representatives to the Central Church Council. When missionaries are on the field, the Central Church Council usually meets at the same time as the Field Council, and matters of common interest—including the assignment of missionaries—are decided together.

The scheme in Kenya is almost exactly parallel, except that the Districts are there called Regions. At the insistence of the Africans, missionaries still have a place on the councils of the church.

In Tanzania, a different form of church government was adopted. This provided for a large Synod with representatives from all parts of the field, which met once a year. A small Executive Committee carried on church affairs between the meetings of the Synod, and developed into a hierarchy. Generally speaking there is an excellent spirit of co-operation between the churches and the missionaries; but there have been differences of opinion between the Executive Committee and the Mission. Relations have, however, been happier recently.

In all the fields the Lord has raised up men of God in the African church, men of wisdom and discernment. Most of these men have had little in the way of education. They have been to Bible School for three or four years, and have gained a remarkable knowledge of the Scriptures. Hundreds of evangelists and pastors have been trained in the nine such schools throughout our fields, and they are doing good work, many in remote places.

But good as they are, the rising standard of education has left them behind. More highly trained pastors are needed to reach today's young people. There are two higher grade Theological Colleges in our fields. There is one which is a co-operative effort between the A.I.M., the Unevangelized Fields Mission and other like-minded societies in north-east Congo.

In Kenya there is the Scott Theological College at Machakos. Here an advanced course is followed. Up to the present there has not been a large number of students, but those who graduate are trained to take a leading place in church life.

31

Other Activities

I. LITERATURE

THE Africans are becoming literate. They can read. They *will* read. But what? With the voracious appetite which is the result of education, they will read anything and everything that comes their way. Subversive literature abounds in East Africa, colourful and well produced. Christian literature needs to be searched for.

There is, of course, the Bible. The Word of God in part or in whole has been translated into many of the leading languages. This has involved sweat and toil and tears. In some cases the languages had to be drawn out from the people word by word and the grammar deduced. In others, work done by early pioneers had to be revised in the light of later knowledge. This meant much painstaking concentration, followed by the chore of typing and retyping. This continues today. The Lugbara Bible is just off the press. Work is still being done in Azande, Luo, Masai, Turkana, Pokot, Kakwa and other languages.

When translated, the Scriptures are printed by the Bible Societies, who subsidize the well-bound volumes they produce so that they may be within the reach of all. The Scripture Gift Mission provides booklets of texts for free distribution. To these societies and to others, all Missions owe a great debt of thanks. The African churches understand and appreciate these services.

But other literature is needed, and this, for the most part, is printed on Mission presses. There were three print-shops, as well as a small press at Arua. It has not yet been possible to reopen the one at Rethy in Congo since the troubles there, owing to lack of personnel. Those at Bwiru (near Mwanza) in Tanzania and at Kijabe in Kenya are both well-equipped modern shops, with experienced missionary printers in charge, assisted by Africans they have trained. Behind these are writers, editors, artists and photographers. On these presses tracts, Sunday School lessons, Bible Instruction booklets and other helpful literature are turned out in great numbers.

At Kijabe a monthly journal in Swahili is produced. This goes under the title *Afrika ya Kesho (The Africa of Tomorrow)*. Many of these go to students overseas, but most are sold in Kenya and Tanzania. In order to keep the price down, the magazine has to be subsidized. A similar paper in simple English is also issued.

It is one thing to produce these various publications, and another to sell them. Sales promotion calls for a department on its own. But few can be spared for this important task. Bookshops have been opened in Kenya, Tanzania, Uganda and Congo. A number of bookmobiles visit remoter areas in all these countries. These are well patronized and stocks of Bibles and Scripture portions they carry are often sold out in a surprisingly short time. At the important agricultural shows held in Kenya, book-stalls are arranged. In addition to the sale of many books, valuable contacts for Christ are made.

Much more literature could be sold if only there were personnel available and gifted at sales promotion. The whole countryside in Kenya, Tanzania and Uganda is peppered with little shops owned by Africans or Asians. If only these could be persuaded to stock Christian literature, sales would escalate rapidly. Much more could be done in the towns also.

II. Missionaries' Children

Both by example and precept, Mr. Hurlburt, from the earliest days, encouraged missionaries to marry and have families. A problem arose, however, when the children needed education. It seemed a needless hardship on both parents and children if, working in a healthy climate, it was necessary to be parted in early days. In view of this, schools for the children of missionaries formed a part of missionary activities.

The first was commenced at Kijabe and was already well established before ex-President Theodore Roosevelt laid the foundation stone of a new building for it in 1908. Many have contributed to the development of Rift Valley Academy. From its very elementary character in the early years it has now developed into a large institution with over three hundred pupils, most of whom are residents.

Mr. Downing's son Herbert, and his wife, have devoted themselves to this task for many years. At first only primary education was given, but its range has been increased gradually until it now covers full high school. When its pupils leave the Academy and go to America they are able to take their places among those who have had good high-school teaching in that country and to continue their studies without handicap. Most of them maintain a bright testimony for Christ and make good. A surprisingly large percentage enter the Lord's service when their training is completed. Many find their way into the ranks of the A.I.M. Others go to different Mission fields or take up ministry at home.

The American curriculum is followed. Attempts have been made more than once to introduce a stream which would prepare students for entrance into British schools; but each time it has been found impracticable and abandoned.

Music has featured prominently in school activities. The Rift Valley Choir is justly celebrated and has appeared both on the Kenya Sound and Television broadcasts, as well as giving concerts in aid of charities. It has been congratulated by President Jomo Kenyatta personally.

When the school was small, it catered for the children of settlers as well as for those of missionaries. As it has grown, however, and applications have come from other Missions, provision has had to be limited to the children of missionaries, but selected children of Africans are also admitted.

A similar Academy is situated at Rethy in the Congo. This began about forty years ago, but it was not properly organized until Professor Winsor became its Principal. He had no easy task, but thanks mainly to his efforts in those early days, the school is now well established. Only in recent years has Rethy Academy taken its scholars to the level of junior high school. When they have graduated from that, it is usual for them to be fed into the Rift Valley Academy.

Victoria Academy, Nassa, in Tanzania, has never had more than a few pupils, and has not taken them beyond the elementary stage, when they go to Kijabe.

Most children of British missionaries have gone to government or private schools in Kenya, where the British curriculum is followed. These are not usually able to have the same spiritual help as that given in the Mission schools; but having to make a stand for Christ in the midst of others has often produced strong Christians.

EPILOGUE

So a garden has been produced in Inland Africa. Indeed, it is a cluster of gardens, each bearing fruit in its own way and measure. No longer is the seed foreign. Planted by Peter Cameron Scott and his band of pioneers, fostered by a succession of gardeners, watered by the prayers of faithful supporters in the homelands, it has become indigenous.

This has been brought about by a series of miracles. The chronicles reveal God's intervention in special ways in connection with the advances in each field. A few have been recorded in these pages; but who can recount the whole? On every field, on each station and in the churches far off in the bush, God has been manifestly at work.

A succession of gardeners of God's choice, called in individual ways, trained and prepared, have been provided for and sustained. As they have gone to work, again and again they have found themselves facing seeming impossibilities and tasks beyond their powers. Yet, in answer to prayer, ability has been given, closed doors have been opened, needs have been supplied, adversaries have been overcome and, in many cases, gloriously saved. Doctors have seen results on patients which no modern drug or the most skilful surgery could produce. Enemies have become friends. Witch-doctors have renounced their dark practices and burned their paraphernalia. Lives have been changed and, when times of testing and persecution have come, they have borne fearless testimony to their faith and have stood firm. Many, men and women, young and old, have been beaten, cursed, disinherited and, in some cases, have laid down their lives rather than deny the One Who has saved them, given peace instead of fear, love for hatred and joy for mourning.

In short, God has been at work. The seed is no longer imported; it has taken root. Its propagation is now in the hands of national believers.

May expatriate gardeners now be dispensed with? The countries are now independent and standing on their own feet; cannot the churches carry on without missionary help?

The troubles in Congo, necessitating the withdrawal of all Europeans, demonstrated that the churches can, if necessary, stand without them. Is their presence therefore unnecessary?

Ask the nationals. The answer is the same whether the question is asked in Kenya, Tanzania, Congo, Uganda, Central African Republic or Sudan:

'Send us missionaries! Missionary partners! We are willing to do what we can, but there are many things we cannot do yet.'

They ask for those who will teach them more of the Word of God, in Bible School, Short-term Bible Courses or Theological College. Few Africans are qualified for this.

Not sufficient nationals are yet competent to teach in the secondary schools which are springing up in such large numbers. Most of the teachers must come from overseas. Religious Instruction is included in the curricula and this provides unparalleled opportunities for Christian teachers to give regular instruction in the things of God to the rising generation.

It will be many years before there are sufficient African doctors and nurses to staff the hospitals and dispensaries. The churches call for help in this too. Medical work presents wide open doors of service. In the half-million square miles for which the A.I.M. is responsible, there are twelve hospitals, only eight of which are functioning as such at present. To staff these and to supervise the dispensaries dependent on them, there are fifteen doctors, including those on furlough. Nurses as well as doctors are in very short supply.

They need help also in the vast field of literature—its preparation, printing, publication and distribution. This is an area of limitless scope, only lightly touched.

There is a clamant call for work among youth, among students in colleges and universities, and these need people who are specially qualified.

And so we might continue. They are still needed—those who will go out in partnership with the Church, working under its leadership if necessary. Such can be assured of the heartiest of welcomes. But they must be men and women who have been truly called of God, Spirit-filled, humble and prepared for anything. Such are the gardeners whom God will use to continue this work of miracle with the Church—tender of touch with the young plants, generous in enriching the soil, supporting, encouraging the growth.

Coupled, however, with these great needs is the urgent necessity for strong support at home—an army of those who will engage in the hidden and unheralded work of intercession; dedicated souls who will busy themselves in the ministry of prayer, praying regularly and faithfully, definite and informed prayers, and who will enlist others in this profitable and essential task. They can touch Africa, though they may never see the field or the people for whom they pray; they walk by faith, not by sight.

But miracles will happen in answer.

Those who serve in the various Home Offices of the Mission get a glimpse of the miracles along one line. These serve sacrificially, often giving long hours, bearing burdens and coping with emergencies. The Mission and the missionaries are deeply indebted to them. They are cheered on their way from time to time as they see prayers answered in the supply of needed funds and offers of service. But rich eternal reward awaits them.

God has been at work throughout the history of the Africa Inland Mission. Conditions today call for a continuance of miracle. It comes as the Lord's people pray.

AFRICA INLAND MISSION

BRITISH HOME COUNCIL
43 Blackstock Road, London N.4.

AMERICAN HOME COUNCIL
253 Henry Street, Brooklyn, N.Y. 11201, U.S.A.

AUSTRALIAN HOME COUNCIL
62a Chisholm Road, Auburn, New South Wales, Australia.

CANADIAN HOME COUNCIL
3 Rowanwood Avenue, Toronto 5, Ontario, Canada.

SOUTH AFRICAN COMMITTEE
P.O. Box 3644, Cape Town, South Africa.